# BUILDING DANCES

## SECOND EDITION

Susan McGreevy-Nichols
Helene Scheff, RDE
Marty Sprague, MA

**Human Kinetics**

**Library of Congress Cataloging-in-Publication Data**

McGreevy-Nichols, Susan, 1952-
    Building dances: a guide to putting movements together/Susan McGreevy-Nichols, Helene Scheff, and Marty Sprague—2nd ed.
        p. cm.
    ISBN 0-7360-5089-2 (soft cover)
    1. Dance for children—Study and teaching (Elementary). 2. Dance—Study and teaching (Secondary) 3. Choreography—Study and teaching (Elementary) 4. Choreography—Study and teaching (Secondary) 5. Movement education. I. Scheff, Helene, 1939- II. Sprague, Marty, 1950-  III. Title.
    GV1799.M3    2005
    792.2'083--dc22                                                              2004017895

ISBN: 0-7360-5089-2

**Acquisitions Editor:** Judy Patterson Wright, PhD; **Developmental Editor:** Melissa Feld; **Assistant Editor:** Kathleen D. Bernard, Ragen Sanner; **Copyeditor:** Jan Feeney; **Proofreader:** Amie Bell; **Permission Manager:** Dalene Reeder; **Graphic Designer:** Andrew Tietz; **Graphic Artist:** Yvonne Griffith; **Cover Designer:** Jack W. Davis; **Art Manager:** Kelly Hendren; **Illustrator:** Dick Flood; **Diagrams:** Craig Ronto; **Printer (book):** Versa Press; **Printer (Deal a Dance card deck):** MultiAd

Printed in the United States of America          10   9   8   7   6   5   4   3   2   1

**Human Kinetics**
Web site: www.HumanKinetics.com

*United States:* Human Kinetics, P.O. Box 5076, Champaign, IL 61825-5076
800-747-4457
e-mail: humank@hkusa.com

*Canada:* Human Kinetics, 475 Devonshire Road Unit 100, Windsor, ON N8Y 2L5
800-465-7301 (in Canada only)
e-mail: orders@hkcanada.com

*Europe:* Human Kinetics, 107 Bradford Road, Stanningley, Leeds LS28 6AT, United Kingdom
+44 (0) 113 255 5665
e-mail: hk@hkeurope.com

*Australia:* Human Kinetics, 57A Price Avenue, Lower Mitcham, South Australia 5062
08 8277 1555
e-mail: liaw@hkaustralia.com

*New Zealand:* Human Kinetics, Division of Sports Distributors NZ Ltd.
P.O. Box 300 226 Albany, North Shore City, Auckland
0064 9 448 1207
e-mail: blairc@hknewz.com

# CONTENTS

# PREFACE

The importance of dance as an educational tool has become more apparent to many educators since we wrote the first edition of *Building Dances* in 1995. The process of building dances (choreography) involves much more than putting movements together. Students who have had the opportunity to experience this process learn life skills while they learn to enjoy movement for its own sake. In these times of couch potatoes, children need to experience that moving is good for the body, the mind, and the creative spirit.

We are proud to bring you this second edition of *Building Dances.* Many people have embraced the materials we presented to you in the first edition. We have received many notes about how you are making these materials work for you and your students. So, why a second edition? We have included new material, updated material, and in some cases, more in-depth material. (See the "Special Features" section of "How to Use This Book" for details on these additions and changes.)

If this is your first encounter with *Building Dances,* welcome! We know that when you use the tools in this book to encourage your students to create dances, you will become more comfortable with the process yourself.

Think of *Building Dances* as your architect's manual, a novice's guide to choreography. The necessary tools and building materials are here. All you need to add to the 15 dance construction models are the students. Each construction model guides you through the activity to help you maximize its use. Use your students' input and ideas as architectural details, the fancy scrollwork, and the impressive facade. Don't be afraid to experiment. If all the foundational materials are in place, the building will not fall, and you will be successful. There is no wrong way! Nothing is as rewarding as seeing students at any level bring a concept through the dance-building process under your guidance. When you make a game or puzzle of the dance construction process, you and your students benefit from a creative experience that challenges critical-thinking skills and the artistic impulse.

*Dance* means to move one's feet or body, or both, rhythmically in a pattern of steps, especially to the accompaniment of music. But dance isn't just that; dance is movement created and executed to satisfy a need. It can be stylized. It can be done with or without musical accompaniment. It can tell a story or simply be abstract patterns. It can create images, use space, define moods, and create and channel energy. The 15 dance construction models in this book enable the dance movements to take on a shape, create a scene, communicate a story, foster an idea, and interpret a piece of music. These movements, which are created through the use of dance construction models, can use the entire body or various body parts in isolation. They can range from very basic movements (such as walking, sitting, and arm waving) to more complicated dance movements (such as leaps and turns). A dance, the result of a lesson using a dance construction model, can move simply in one direction or use an intricate floor pattern.

In both private and public education, dance is an underserved discipline. It constantly gets caught between the cracks. Where does it belong in the established subject areas? Ideally, it should be treated as a separate entity taught by certified dance educators or dance specialists. In actuality, a national survey showed that the majority of responsibility of teaching dance falls to physical educators, theater or English teachers, music educators, and classroom teachers. With new developments in the educational arena, most high school students need a certain number of performing arts credits as a graduation requirement. With the cutbacks in funding for hiring teachers, this responsibility falls to those already on staff. This could be you!

The dance construction models in this book were developed to satisfy the needs expressed by five constituencies: physical education teachers, drama teachers and coaches, classroom teachers, music teachers, and dance teachers. We saw an even wider range of people who could use these models in many ways: recreation and community center personnel who desire to have students experience the joy of moving in a variety of ways and of creating their own dances. Many colleges and universities are using *Building Dances* as a requirement for courses in teacher preparation for physical education and dance. Many of these dance construction models have been successfully presented at conferences to several of the constituencies mentioned here. In addition, these models have been tested on children from grades kindergarten to 12, all of whom have proven to be receptive participants. Children love to perform and, given the opportunity, will amaze you with their ability. By creating a dance in each of your classes, you will have enough material to put on a dance performance that will charm students, teachers, and parents alike. Read on to see how you can use this book to challenge your students!

# ACKNOWLEDGMENTS

The second edition of *Building Dances* is a testimony to all the educators and students who have successfully added teaching and learning dance to their list of accomplishments. We thank you all! We thank the attendees of AAHPERD, RIAHPERD, NASPE, NAEYC, NMSA, NELMS, NJAAPERD, MAHPERD (Maine, Massachusetts, and Maryland, IRA, Home Schooling Association, Department of Defense) NDEO, and NHAHPERD conferences over the years who have been so open about adopting a new way of doing things. We are also grateful to the people at Human Kinetics who have the wisdom to see that, indeed, dance should be part of every student's learning experience.

# BLUEPRINTS FOR BUILDING A DANCE: HOW TO USE THIS BOOK

If you've never done it before, the thought of creating your own dance from scratch can be very intimidating. Just like building a house, building a dance (as choreography has been called) can be a manageable and even fun process when you have the proper tools, some basic skills, and a plan. This book is designed as a blueprint to guide you and your students through the process of building a dance.

## Special Features

This book is unique because it is a hands-on tool that invites and cultivates variety and creativity within given structures. Each section of the book is summarized for easy reference. A glossary explains many special dance terms in everyday language. Also included in this edition is an appendix that lists national standards for dance and physical education. The chapter on assessment (chapter 6) is updated as well. New forms and checklists make the assessment process easier for you and your students. Parts of a lesson, lesson plans, and student assessment forms are included. The unique Deal a Dance card deck (with 230 movement examples) can be used as a teacher's guide or as an interactive classroom tool to stimulate your students' imaginations as they build their dances. Journal entries from chapter 5 and assessment checklists from chapter 6 can be found on cards 232-246. The "Try This" suggestions give students basic skills and knowledge. These revised cards also include challenges that take the students into higher levels of application and creativity. An "Ask Yourself" (student reflection) section helps the students evaluate their own work.

In chapter 1, "Laying a Foundation," you will be introduced to the relationship between creativity and choreography. You will learn ways to facilitate creativity, explore the three parts of a lesson, and examine three sample lesson plans. In chapter 2, "Identifying Building Supplies," you will become acquainted with movement skills and elements, ethnic and cultural influences, historical and social perspectives, sources of music, and ways of organizing music to facilitate choreography. All these materials and tools assist students in the choreographic process.

Chapter 3, "Constructing the Frame and Roof," familiarizes you with structures of dances and choreographic forms; story lines and characterizations as the basis for some dances; and the use of sound, props, costumes, scenery, and set pieces to enhance choreography. We also give you some tools for mounting a full production. Chapter 4, "Adding Architectural Details," explains and clarifies the use of accenting, gestures, stylizing, and expressive qualities in the choreographic process. Chapter 5, "Putting It All Together," leads you through the seven steps to building a dance, from the birth of an idea to the performance.

Chapter 6, "Inspecting Your Creation," gives you another set of blueprints; these are for evaluation and assessment. Finally, chapter 7, "Building Dances From Blueprints," supplies 15 fun ways of implementing choreography through dance construction models. With the use of basic skills and concepts, each construction model is a nonthreatening learning experience for both teachers and students. Each one addresses specific developmental skills and encourages some aspect of the creative process. The teacher assumes the role of facilitator, not necessarily demonstrator. A description of the activity or procedure, a sample activity, grade level suggestions, and criteria for assessment are included in each activity. These sections guide the facilitator in maximizing the learning experience. Communicating with the students is a constant source of inspiration. Their willingness to cooperate and bring their thoughts and ideas to the class make every class a rewarding and exciting experience.

In chapter 7, any of the dance construction models can be used in a single lesson, as a dance unit, as a full-semester course, or as a yearlong program. They can also be used in building a dance curriculum. The following is a description of each dance construction model:

- *Deal a Dance* has as its structural support a series of 115 playing cards that are divided into four categories: Dance Technique, Elements That Change Movements, Sports and Game Movements, and Creative Movement Suggestions. The information on both the front and the back of these playing cards (230 movement examples) provides the raw material you need in working with all the construction models. The cards describe the basic movement skills and elements for facilitating choreography. The versatility of the cards makes every dance class an adventure.

- *Picture Dance* uses pictures as a source of positions and movements for creating dances.
- *Words, Sentences, and Paragraphs* bridges the gap between language and movement and provide opportunities for team teaching with classroom teachers.
- *Story Dance* invites a three-dimensional interpretation of literature and hones storytelling skills.
- *Write What I See* develops observation and writing skills.
- *Machine Dance* fosters cooperative learning through the creation of imaginary, visual robotics. It also can introduce the use of sounds to enhance the creative process.
- *Costume and Prop Dance* uses articles of clothing and small, handheld items to play on preconceived notions and attitudes in order to help students get started and become more comfortable with moving in creative ways.
- *Decode a Dance* introduces aesthetic criticism as a means of understanding dance as an art form.
- *Create a Culture* adds a new twist to multicultural education and can play a significant role in the understanding of aspects of a culture.
- *On the Move Dance* develops an awareness of modes of transportation through their relationship to movement.
- *Holiday Dance* brings celebrations and traditions to life and helps students understand why dance is important to so many ethnic groups and cultures.
- *Out of This World* helps students explore the solar system and the movement inherent in space.
- *Four Seasons* celebrates the four seasons and the cycles of life within those seasons.
- *Animal Kingdom* encourages the study of animals as students create dances portraying the world from the animals' point of view.
- *It's All Around Us* helps students understand their environment, the impact they have on it, and the effect it has on them.

# Threefold Purpose

The focus of this book is to demystify the process of choreography and to help you find a comfort zone that will enable you to teach the process within a dance unit. Our approach puts the educator in the role of facilitator rather than demonstrator—one who is responsible for making something take place. Using the dance construction models detailed in this book, you as the teacher explain the material, teach the necessary skills, review the procedure, direct the action, analyze the results, and assess the outcomes, while the students do the creative work.

Second, this book is a reference tool that introduces the basics of choreography through a series of developmentally appropriate dance construction models; it is applicable to any grade K-12 situation. Our aim is for you to use the material in this book to "dangle a carrot in front of a donkey's nose," inspiring users to want to learn more. We hope you will become excited about choreography and dance and therefore will want to bring professionals into your facility to choreograph and interact with your students.

Third, this book can fulfill many of the dance content standards as part of the National Standards for Arts Education. With the passage of the Goals 2000: Educate America Act, the arts are written into federal law and acknowledged as a core subject. Title II of the act addresses the issue of education standards. In 1992, the Consortium of National Arts Education Associations developed the National Education Standards for the Arts as a guide to help teachers identify children's expected knowledge and competence in the arts. The resulting book, *National Standards for the Arts Education: What Every Young American Should Know and Be Able to Do in the Arts,* is available for purchase through the Music Educators National Conference by calling 800-828-0229. The latter addresses the standards not only for dance but also for music, theater, and the visual arts. The national standards for dance appear in the appendix of this book. *The National Standards for the Arts Education* booklet can be obtained by ordering through AAHPERD Publications, P.O. Box 385, Oxon Hill, MD 20750-0385. Their phone number is 800-321-0789. The activities in *Building Dances* also fulfill many of the physical education content standards as part of the National Standards for Physical Education, which are also included in the appendix. To order a copy of the new edition of *Moving into the Future: National Standards for Physical Education,* second edition, visit the online bookstore at www.naspeinfo.org or call 800-321-0789. Within each content standard are achievement standards that specify the levels of understanding and achievement that students are expected to attain at the completion of grades 4, 8, and 12. The resulting framework can function as a guide when you're designing a comprehensive dance program.

You can use *Building Dances* to satisfy the various content standards. For example, Deal a Dance (found in chapter 7 and in the attached card deck) can be used in grades K to 4 to teach children various locomotor and nonlocomotor movements and dance elements, in grades 5 to 8 to help students combine movements to create simple dances and to use dance as a way to communicate meaning, and in grades 9 to 12 to help students understand and apply various choreographic principles as the students are engaged in the creative process. Students can discuss what they like about the dances and how they can change them.

Other examples include using Create a Culture (in chapter 7) to foster discussion among middle school students about their own cultures as they create an expression of their own invented culture. Or, you might select the Story Dance (chapter 7) to help students use dance to create meaningful communication as well as make connections to drama, art, and writing when they create an original children's story with costumes, scenery, advertisements, program booklets, and reviews. The students could perform their stories for a neighborhood elementary school or recreation center. Use the performance checklist (found in chapter 6) to help you evaluate the piece.

Whether you're a physical education teacher, drama teacher or coach, music teacher, dance teacher, classroom teacher, or recreation specialist, this book is for you. Use it to help students experience both the joy of moving in a variety of ways and the satisfaction of creating their own dances.

# Chapter 1

# Laying a Foundation: Basic Building Blocks

In this chapter you will find the tools to answer the following questions:

- What makes a dance?
- What is the relationship between creativity and choreography?
- How is creativity facilitated?
- What is the structure of a dance class?
- What are the three parts of a dance?

As with any construction, it is important to start by laying a strong foundation to avoid having the structure fall apart. In dance, when you lay a foundation you use knowledge of movement skills, movement elements, and the principles of choreography. Choreography is a creative process. This creative process can be facilitated and taught. Other structures addressed in this chapter are the structures of a dance class and the three parts of a dance.

## What Makes a Dance?

Communication through movement should be the goal when building a dance. When we teach students we often use a literary model. We tell them that movements are like words. You put words together to make sentences. In dance these sentences are called dance phrases. Sentences are put together to make paragraphs in the same way that dance phrases are linked to make sections. Sections, when linked together, make a dance.

## Relationship Between Creativity and Choreography

Choreography is the art of building dances, and the choreographer is the architect. Creativity figures strongly in this building process—the more creative, inventive, and flexible the choreographer, the more versatile the dance. Once you become comfortable building simple dances, with creativity you can make them more complex. A sense of adventure and imagination makes the sky the limit.

Begin the creative process by learning to organize your thoughts and materials. Small starts and steps can lead to wonderful choreography. Remember that choreography can evolve and change, and there is no one right solution.

Creativity doesn't mean that thoughts and gestures are pulled from the air in an unorganized manner. Two methods that facilitate creativity are the use of imagery and brainstorming. Imagery can be invaluable in helping you envision what a movement should look like. The following are sample questions to stimulate imagery and creativity:

- What does a snowflake look like as it falls to the ground?
- How do tree branches look on a mild, breezy day? Or in a hurricane? (See figure 1.1.)
- What do you see when you think of a schoolyard full of children?

**FIGURE 1.1**  Some trees are calm and flowing. Others move more sharply in response to the elements.

Brainstorming is a problem-solving strategy. Gathering information through unrestricted and spontaneous discussion stimulates creative thinking and aids in developing new ideas or ways of solving a choreographic problem. Use the following steps to facilitate creativity:

| STEP | EXAMPLE |
| --- | --- |
| 1. Determine problem. | Create a dance showing conflict. |
| 2. Brainstorm. | Discuss the following: What constitutes a conflict? What does your body feel like during conflict? What image pops into your mind when you think of conflict? What gestures would you use during a confrontation? What facial expressions denote a conflict? Would the movements be smooth or sharp, fast or slow, small or large? |
| 3. Improvise and explore movement possibilities. | To improvise is to compose without preparation or forethought or on the spot, without movement being |

directed. The dancers move in ways that they believe best tell their feelings or story. Improvisation can also result from listening to the music and reacting from within. Use improvisation to create three movements: one that moves from place to place, a second frozen in place (pose), and a third that must turn. All moves must convey conflict.

4. Develop choreography.     Link the three movements and repeat the series three times in a row.

Use these steps with any subject matter or abstract idea.

## Three Parts of a Lesson

A typical dance class has three sections: warm-up, activity, and cool-down. The general information that follows serves as a support structure for lesson planning.

### Warm-Up

Although as educators and adults we know the value and necessity of a proper warm-up before any physical activity, we must stress to our students the importance of a careful warm-up. Children are taught that warming up the muscles before a football, baseball, or soccer game or stretching before running or jogging is necessary and beneficial. And because dance is also a physical activity, dance educators should emphasize that warming up is equally important before dancing.

Because children tend to be impressed by visuals and imagery, you can relate the following comparisons to "cold" muscles:

• **Example 1:** Ask the students if they have ever handled Silly Putty. You might ask, "How difficult is it to pull the putty when it is cold, and what happens when you try to stretch it quickly?" (It snaps in two.) Then ask them what happens after you warm the putty in your hand for several minutes. (You suddenly find that it is pliable and offers little resistance to stretching.) Explain that human muscle is like Silly Putty and that taking the time to warm the muscles before exercising makes them more efficient and easier to use.

- **Example 2:** Tap dancers (hoofers) once thought they didn't have to warm up. After all, they really didn't stretch or exert their muscles. The late Sammy Davis Jr. once said that if he had known of the need for proper warm-up and had done so regularly, he probably wouldn't have needed hip-replacement surgery.

Students should know what is needed for a complete warm-up. The following foundation-building components should be included, in the order listed:

1. Lubricate each joint, exploring full range of motion and using gentle movements.
2. Use aerobic movements—repetitive movements that bring blood flow to large muscle groups. Only when there is adequate blood flow to the muscles can you begin to stretch.
3. Stretch large muscle groups.
4. Use crunches and curl-downs for abdominal strength. Curl-downs start from a seated position with knees bent and feet planted firmly on the floor. You then slowly roll the spine down to the floor. (These could also be done at the beginning of a cool-down instead of the end of a warm-up.)

## Activity

Whichever activity you select as the focus of your lesson, use the following general progression:

1. Introduce a movement skill. This is a physical skill that includes both locomotor and nonlocomotor movement. A broader explanation and examples can be found in chapter 2.
2. Introduce a movement element. This term defines how and where a movement is done. A broader explanation can be found in chapter 2.
3. Create a movement pattern or sequence using skills and elements. This is where students can learn some important information about dance and choreography. Their work may involve learning and memorizing a teacher's movement.
4. Have students explore the use of movement skills and elements using problem-solving techniques.

## Cool-Down

Use the cool-down segment of your lesson to accomplish the following:

1. After strenuous activity the muscles and cardiovascular system need to return to normal. Students should continue a slow activity until their breathing and heart rate are normal.

2. Students need a calming conclusion to the physical activity before returning to their academic activities.

3. During this time, students and teachers can reflect on the lesson of the day and on what everyone has learned.

# Safety Tips

Stress the following safety practices at every level during all warm-up and dance activities.

1. When doing knee bends (pliés), keep the knees over the toes.

2. When doing any kind of jump, start from bent knees (plié) and land with bent knees (in plié).

3. Align the spine properly in every exercise. Avoid a hyperextended back or a forward-thrust pelvis.

4. Always make sure there is adequate blood flow to the muscles before stretching.

5. Make sure shoulders are relaxed and pulled down.

6. If during any movement throughout the lesson you feel pain, stop immediately.

7. Take time to cool down by continuing to walk. (Different students' heart rates return to normal at different times. Encourage students to take whatever time they need to cool down adequately and to be aware and in charge of their own bodies.)

# Three Sample Lesson Plans

## Warm-Up

This teacher-facilitated warm-up is designed to give children the necessary tools to create their own developmentally correct warm-ups for future use. Before beginning a warm-up, lay down the ground rules: Make no sharp movements of the neck, always make the knees face the same direction as the toes, and make movements gentle.

1. The lubrication portion of the warm-up includes an inventory of the joints and muscles and an exploration of how they can be moved.

GRADES K TO 4

Starting with the top of the body, ask the students how many ways they can move their body parts:

- Head and neck
- Shoulders
- Arms, elbows, and wrists
- Torso
- Hips and legs
- Knees, ankles, and feet

(This exploration can also be done from bottom to top.)

2. The aerobic portion of a warm-up includes
   - alternate jogging in place and freezing,
   - alternate hopping and freezing,
   - alternate jumping and freezing, and
   - alternate skipping and freezing.

3. You can begin the stretch portion of the warm-up by asking students how they can
   - make their bodies taller,
   - make their arms reach the ceiling,
   - make their arms reach the side walls, and
   - make their hands touch their toes and then try to straighten their knees.

## Activity

1. Select and teach three movement skills:
   - Run (card 59)
   - Slide (card 17)
   - Twist (card 67)

2. Introduce and explore an aspect of the movement element of force—strong or weak:
   - Run like a football player.
   - Run like your legs are made of marshmallows.
   - While standing still, make your body look strong.
   - While standing still, make your body look weak.
   - Change the feeling in your muscles to show that they are strong or weak.

3. Develop a small movement pattern using the three movement skills and the movement elements. For example, ask students to slide, twist, and melt down weakly or rise up strongly and run.

## Cool-Down

Choose one of the following, depending on how vigorous the class was:

1.  Stand the students in a circle and have them
    *   place their arms out or on their hips;
    *   put their chins on their chests and breathe deeply, raising their heads as they inhale and lowering their heads as they exhale; and
    *   raise their arms up to their sides as they inhale and lower them as they exhale.
2.  Discuss the day's activities with students, including what seemed important to them and what they think they should remember.

## Warm-Up

1.  The lubrication portion of the warm-up should include an inventory of the joints and muscles and an exploration of how they can be moved. Starting with the top of the body, ask the students how many ways they can move their body parts:
    *   Head and neck
    *   Shoulders
    *   Arms, elbows, and wrists
    *   Torso
    *   Hips and legs
    *   Knees, ankles, and feet

    (This exploration can also be done from bottom to top.)
2.  The aerobic portion of the warm-up is called the "fraction" warm-up because it teaches directional signals using mathematics. Students face forward with their feet comfortably apart. They will change directions every eight counts using small jumps in place and jump turns. The teacher is the caller, and the students jump simultaneously with the call.

    A sample series of calls follows:

    **Caller** (counts aloud) 1, 2, 3, 4, quarter (5), turn (6), to the (7), right (8).

    **Students** jump in place for the 8 counts. On the first count of the next 8-count pattern, the students execute the quarter turn as commanded.

    **Caller** (counts aloud) 1, 2, 3, 4, half (5), turn (6), to the (7), left (8).

**Students,** facing new direction, jump in place for the second 8 counts, and then execute a half turn as commanded on the first count of the next 8-count pattern.

**Caller** (counts aloud) 1, 2, 3, 4, three-quarter (5), turn (6), to the (7), left (8).

**Students,** facing new direction, jump in place for the third set of 8 counts, and then execute a three-quarter turn as commanded on the first count of the next 8-count pattern.

Note: Always continue the activity from the direction that was last called.

This activity, in addition to being aerobic, sharpens listening skills and teaches math skills.

3. Begin the stretch portion of the warm-up by asking students how they can
   - make their bodies taller,
   - make their arms reach the ceiling,
   - make their arms reach the side walls,
   - make their hands touch their toes while they try to straighten their knees, and
   - make their muscles feel and become longer.

Also ask students how they can do these stretches while sitting or lying on the floor.

## Activity

1. Select and teach the following three movement skills:
   - Three-step turn (card 61)
   - Kick (card 45)
   - Leap (card 4)
2. Introduce and explore an aspect of the movement element of space—change of direction #1 (card 148).
3. Develop a small movement pattern using the three movement skills and the movement element. For example, ask students to do a three-step turn, run and leap, and kick (letting the kick change their direction).

## Cool-Down

Choose one or more of the following to be included in your cool-down, depending on the class activities:

1. Students stand in a circle and
   - place their arms out or on their hips;

- put their chins on their chests and breathe deeply, raising their heads as they inhale and lowering their heads as they exhale;
- raise their arms up to their sides as they inhale and lower them as they exhale; and
- roll the body down to a limp, folded-over position while exhaling and then bring it to an erect, shoulder-squared position while inhaling.

2. Discuss the day's activities with students, including what seemed important to them and what they think they should remember.

## Warm-Up

1. The lubrication portion of the warm-up includes an inventory of the joints and muscles and an exploration of how they can be moved. Starting with the top of the body, ask the students how many ways they can move their body parts:
   - Head and neck
   - Shoulders
   - Arms, elbows, and wrists
   - Torso
   - Hips and legs
   - Knees, ankles, and feet

   (This exploration can also be done from bottom to top.)

2. Begin the aerobic portion of the warm-up by having the students stand in a circle. They then play follow the leader, with each student developing a movement that he or she thinks contributes to the aerobic activity.

3. The stretch portion of the warm-up continues with the students in a circle. They each demonstrate a movement, which the rest of the class follows, that contributes to this section.

## Activity

1. Select and teach three movement skills:
   - Jazz box (card 63)
   - Kick, ball–change (card 32)
   - Wrap turn (card 62)

2. Introduce and explore the movement element of space—use of floor pattern (cards 173, 174, 175, and 176).

3. Combine movement skills and movement elements:
   - Working in small groups, the students create three poses.
   - Combine these poses with the movement skills in the previous list.
   - Perform movement patterns in several different floor patterns.
   - Present the small-group creations to the class.

## Cool-Down

Choose any one or more of the following to be included in your cool-down, depending on the class activities:

1. Students stand in a circle and
   - place their arms out or on their hips;
   - put their chins on their chests and breathe deeply, raising their heads as they inhale and lowering their heads as they exhale;
   - raise their arms up to their sides as they inhale and lower them as they exhale; and
   - roll the body down to a limp, folded-over position while exhaling and then bring it to an erect, shoulder-squared position while inhaling.
2. Discuss the day's activities with students:
   - What part of the lesson seemed important to them?
   - What do they think they should remember?
   - What did they learn?
   - Which of the movement patterns did they enjoy the most, and why?

# Three Parts of a Dance

A well-structured dance has a beginning, a middle, and an end.

## Beginning

The beginning of the dance should be clear and, whatever the choice, should capture the audience's attention. The following are some options:

- Think of the opening as a tableau, a picture, or a painting.
- Start the dance on stage or off.
- Start the dance with music or without, or begin the music before the dance.

## Middle

The middle, or body, of the dance should not lose the audience's attention by being boring or trite. It should be a development of the main idea. The following are among the countless ways to make the middle interesting:

- Vary movement patterns.
- Repeat movement patterns.
- Perform movement patterns at different times.
- Have different groups perform complementary movement patterns simultaneously.
- Vary dancers' positions on the stage.

## End

The conclusion should also be clearly defined:

- If the dance ends "on stage," hold the final pose as though it were a painting.
- Have the dancers leave the stage.
- End the dance with the music, have it continue after the music has ended, or end the dance and have the music continue.

Both the teacher and students should look at the dance with an artist's eye. Most people know what looks good, so remember that aesthetics are in the eye of the beholder.

# Summary

As the instructor or facilitator, you can develop and implement creative lessons. These lessons provide students with foundational skills. You will be able to facilitate creativity and choreography by knowing and understanding what makes a dance, the three parts of a dance, and the three parts of a lesson.

# Chapter 2

# Identifying Building Supplies: Basic Materials for Building Dances

In this chapter you will find the tools to answer the following questions:

- What are movement skills?
- What are movement elements?
- How do cultural influences affect your dance?
- How does knowledge of historical and social perspectives help you make a dance?
- What are three helpful ways of organizing music?

You need basic building blocks and tools to build your dance. These basic abilities are movement skills and elements that all dancers use to create dances. Cultural, social, and historical influences can help you make a dance. Learning how to align your dance with music is another helpful tool in creating dances.

# Movement Skills

All movement, from the everyday activity of walking down the street to the skilled moves of an athlete or dancer, is either locomotor or nonlocomotor. Locomotor movement takes you from one place to another, whereas nonlocomotor movement does not travel through space. Nonlocomotor movement can be either axial or peripheral. Axial is centered on the axis of the body; peripheral movement involves the use of the limbs.

Some basic locomotor movements are

- walking,
- running,
- hopping, and
- jumping.

Other locomotor movements, such as skipping, leaping, galloping, and sliding, are combinations of movements.

Some basic nonlocomotor movements are

- swinging,
- bending,
- stretching,
- twisting, and
- shaking.

Three other nonlocomotor movements that have to do with body parts on the outer edge (peripheral, which can include arm or leg movements) are

- carving (drawing patterns in the air with hands or feet leading),
- spoking (shooting movements from the center of the body outward into space), and
- arcing (hemispheric patterns drawn in the air).

Basic body positions commonly used in physical education classes are also helpful when building dances:

- Tuck position—lying (front, back, side), standing, or sitting
- Pike position—lying, sitting, or standing
- Layout position—lying (front, back) or standing
- Stride position—standing
- Straddle position—standing or sitting

Examples of grade-appropriate movement skills, used alone and in combination, follow. Movements are explained in the glossary and on the Deal a Dance cards.

### Grades K to 4

| | | |
|---|---|---|
| Run | Walk | Skip |
| Leap | Hop | Jump |
| Slide | Crawl | Prance |
| Step–hop | Step, step | Bow |
| One-foot turn | Gallop | Slither |
| Stamp | Thigh slap | Arm circle |
| Sit | Cross legs | Log roll |
| Step and drag | Kneel (two knees) | Lunge |
| Kneel (one knee) | Elbow swing | Kick |
| Knee bend (plié) | Head roll | Scale |
| Flexed foot | Extended foot | Attitude |
| Twist | Arm stretch | March |
| Stand on balls of feet | Butterfly | Side step |

### Grades 5 to 8

| | | |
|---|---|---|
| Jump turns (quarter, half, three-quarter, full) | | Wrap turn |
| Tuck jump | Jazz box | Allemande |
| Three-step turn | Finger snap | Lame-duck step |
| Knee turn | Promenade | Pike jump |
| Ball–change | Pivot turn | Layout jump |
| Stride (jump, turn) | Straddle jump | |

**GRADES 9 TO 12**

| | | |
|---|---|---|
| Grapevine | Knee bend (plié) | Knee fall |
| Seat turn | Lame-duck turn | Pony |
| Bell click | Leap | Stag jump |
| Jazz walk | Kick, ball–change | Triplet |
| Scissors jump | | |

# Movement Elements

Change movements by altering the following elements: shape, space, time, and force. These terms are defined as follows:

• **Shape** involves the positions and ways in which the body is used. Alter shape by changing the position of the body or body parts. The body can be curved or twisted, angular or straight, symmetrical or asymmetrical.

• **Space** is where the movement takes place. Movement can alter the use of space through change of direction (front, side, back, or diagonal), change of facing (face stage right, face stage left, face upstage, face downstage), change of size (large, small), change of level (lying, sitting, kneeling, standing, elevated), change of floor pattern (circle, half circle, zigzag, diagonal line, horizontal and vertical lines), and change of focus (look up, look down, look right, look left, look behind, use multiple focuses).

• **Time** is the length of a movement or a movement pattern. Alter time by changing the speed (tempo) and changing the rhythm (organization of beats).

• **Force** is the quality of the movement or how the movement is performed. Alter force by changing the energy (strong and weak movements), changing the quality (suspended, shaking, collapsed, swinging, percussive, and sustained), and changing the flow of movement (controlled and uncontrolled).

# Celebrating Cultural Diversity

Dance is for everyone, but it means different things to different cultures. In many cultures, dance is not separated from everyday life. It can be used in rites of passage, in giving thanks to the gods, and in the raising and quieting of spirits (figure 2.1). Dance is also a way to celebrate; the movements, meaning, and techniques are handed down from one generation to the next. Men dance with men,

**FIGURE 2.1**   Worshiping the goddess may bring much-needed rain.

women dance with women, and men and women dance together. In many cultures men are not permitted to dance with women or even hold their hands. In some cultures only the men dance. Still in other cultures women are permitted to dance only with other women in the privacy of their chambers. For some dance is intended as an appropriate form of socialization between men and women.

Students can delve into their own and others' cultural backgrounds and find movements and materials to use in building dances. This exploration celebrates cultural diversity, and you can use this exploration to integrate dance into the social studies curriculum. For example, if your students are studying Greece, you can teach them the grapevine step, which is the predominant step in Greek dance. Students can pretend that they are going through and around people and tables at a Greek wedding or feast.

## Historical and Social Perspectives

Dance occurred even in ancient times. History and social studies classes can study how the dances of past and current societies reflect trends and popular cultures of the times. In recent times dance has become a reflection of social customs often dictated by the music of the day. Such vernacular dance, or popular dance done to popular music, is bound by what popular culture will accept. Youth experiment with new dance forms, often to the chagrin of the parents, keepers of the social mores, and people in authority. The minuet of the French courts (figure 2.2) and the waltz of Austria were social dances that did not catch on immediately. The black bottom dance of the Roaring Twenties was thought shocking, but it is now part of history. Likewise, the watusi from the 1960s is now only nostalgia for those who danced their sneakers off during that period. Of course, all this time the Virginia reel, square and line dances, and folk dances from the melting pot of cultures were being kept alive, in part by the physical educators and their students.

Dance as a performing art is also relatively recent. The Greeks in ancient times performed their dances in amphitheaters; in medieval times, madrigal dancers entertained in the streets. Ballet was developed in Europe and was bandied about, and finally one of its main centers was based in France. Hence the vocabulary of ballet is predominantly French. In the early 1900s in the United States, modern dance took hold experimentally with Isadora Duncan and Loie Fuller. The vocabulary for any modern dance was usually in the language of the country where it was being done. However,

**Figure 2.2**   By assuming the proper position, dancers can create the impression of a minuet.

ballet and modern dance now enjoy a commonality—for example, tendu means "stretched foot" in any dance form. Tap evolved into a performing art from African American rhythms and Irish clogging. It is truly an American dance form, along with musical comedy (Broadway show dances) and jazz.

With the increased awareness of the importance of physical fitness, dance has become a physical activity as well as a social one. During a dance workout or class, the muscles, tendons, and ligaments of the body are put to full use, as is the cardiovascular system. Dancing can be a fun way to get in shape and stay fit. Anyone of any age can participate in a dance program as long as it is designed appropriately for the participants' abilities. Preschoolers learn stretching, eye–hand coordination, and basic muscle control; young children add more advanced muscle control and alignment. Teens and young adults learn to refine all those skills and begin to push their bodies' capabilities, aerobically as well as technically. The new concept of dancing for senior citizens includes dance exercises as well as line and square dancing. People of various abilities are doing dance exercises to help keep their bodies in shape and to increase their social interaction. Dance is a social equalizer.

## Who, What, Where, and When of Music

Often we are asked the four Ws about music. A rule to start your thinking is "Simple is Best." The *who* can have many possibilities. You may be working with a cooperating music teacher who has a particular written song or score in mind and would like the students to choreograph a piece to it. You may find that some students come up with a score of percussion sounds to which the dancers react and create. If you are fortunate enough to have an ethnically diverse population, the families of your students might be musicians who can create culturally and ethnically accurate music as a basis for choreography.

The *what* is a more complex issue. You and your students may have differing opinions on what kind of music should be used. The trick is to guide them toward music that will stretch their imaginations and experience, yet will engage them. You can link the music to the subject of their choreography.

*Where* can you find recorded music? We tend to haunt the bargain bins in any store that carries CDs. If titles sound catchy or inspiring, we make the purchase knowing that we can probably find something on the disk that is useful. If you have a particular topic for which you want music, you can do a Web search. Stores that sell recorded music such as Borders or Barnes and Noble also offer online services. They have a large selection of music that fits almost any need, and the selections are listed in such a manner that you can identify specific topics, types, and artists. Some stores even have a feature that allows you to listen to a snippet of some of the bands.

*When* brings us to question the right time to begin to use music. You need to consider the subject of the inspiration. If you or your students have a particular piece of music that has inspired thoughts of choreography, then you might want to begin the process with the music. If you or your students have an idea that stems from a piece of literature or visual art, then the process should start with movement exploration. Later you can play around with different selections that have an appropriate sound. Then you can arrange the movement phrases to fit the music.

# Organizing Music

Music is the mortar that holds a dance together. It can be an integral part of creating dances and can greatly influence a piece of choreography. It can also enhance, encourage, and stimulate the creative process and give dancers a way of creating and remembering choreography. Using music fosters organizational skills by compelling choreographers to think about how the composer uses phrasing, when that phrasing changes, and how to put together combinations and repetitions of movements. Organizing the music makes the task of the choreographer more manageable because it breaks a long piece of music into workable sections. It is then an easier task to fit or adapt the movement to the music.

When music is used, the choreography can represent the feeling, the speed, the rhythm, the phrasing, or the words. Following are three ways of organizing music when building a dance.

## Using Verbal Phrases

Using the words from a piece of music is a simple way to approach choreography. The choreographer selects movements that act out the words, as with pantomime. For example, you organize the music by individual words, sentences, or verbal phrases (such as "the sky is blue"). If you were using "Rock-a-Bye Baby," you could segment the verbal phrases within the music like so ($\frac{6}{8}$ ♪♪♩ ♩ ♪):

Section 1: Rock-a-bye baby

Section 2: on the tree top

Section 3: When the wind blows

Section 4: the cradle will rock

Section 5: When the bough breaks

Section 6: the cradle will fall

Section 7: and down will come baby, cradle and all

You are now able to work with each section, individually, as a separate thought process.

## Counting Beats

Organizing the music by counting beats can also be an effective way of applying music to choreography. Because there are so many styles of music and not everyone is familiar with all of them, the examples used are the nursery rhymes "Three Blind Mice" (see page 22) and "This Old Man" (see page 23). What you see in the first two charts are methods of counting beats (quarter notes) and measures (groups of beats) within musical phrases. Since most novice choreographers don't use written music, we've eliminated actual scores (written music charts) of the songs.

What you see are 8 measures of 4 counts each. Students can clap this 8-measure phrase (32 counts), one clap per beat or count. Make sure that they clap on a hold or rest even though there may not be a word with that note. Conversely, they shouldn't make a clap for every word. Many times several words occur during a single beat. We have also diagrammed a song in 3/4 time, where there are 3 beats to a measure (see page 24). Again, make sure that you clap on a hold or rest, even though a word may not go with that note. You do not need to make a clap for every word.

The method of counting shown for "Three Blind Mice" and "This Old Man" demonstrates where the beats occur. After becoming familiar with the beats in a piece of music, you can then begin the process of organizing it for choreography.

Since most popular music is written in 4/4 time, which means that 4 quarter notes (♩) equal a measure, the two songs that are used as examples are applicable because they, too, are written in 4/4 time,

| Words | ♪ Three | blind | mice | |
|---|---|---|---|---|
| Quarter note | ♪ ♩ | ♩ | ♩ | ♩ |
| Count | ♪ 1 | 2 | 3 | 4 |

| Three | blind | mice | |
|---|---|---|---|
| ♩ | ♩ | ♩ | ♩ |
| 1 | 2 | 3 | 4 |

| See | how | they | run | |
|---|---|---|---|---|
| ♩ | ♩ | ♩ | ♩ |
| 1 | 2 | 3 | 4 |

| See | how | they | run | |
|---|---|---|---|---|
| ♩ | ♩ | ♩ | ♩ |
| 1 | 2 | 3 | 4 |

| They | all | ran | after | the | farmer's | wife |
|---|---|---|---|---|---|---|
| ♩ | | ♩ | | ♩ | ♩ |
| 1 | | 2 | | 3 | 4 |

| She | cut off their | tails with a | carving | knife |
|---|---|---|---|---|
| ♩ | ♩ | ♩ | ♩ |
| 1 | 2 | 3 | 4 |

| Did you ever | see such a | sight in your | life |
|---|---|---|---|
| ♩ | ♩ | ♩ | ♩ |
| 1 | 2 | 3 | 4 |

| As | three | blind | mice | |
|---|---|---|---|---|
| ♩ | ♩ | ♩ | ♩ |
| 1 | 2 | 3 | 4 |

| Words | ▶ This | old | man | he | plays | one |
|---|---|---|---|---|---|---|
| Quarter note | ▶ ♩ | | ♩ | ♩ | | ♩ |
| Count | ▶ 1 | | 2 | 3 | | 4 |

| He | plays | knickknack | on | my | thumb |
|---|---|---|---|---|---|
| ♩ | | ♩ | ♩ | | ♩ |
| 1 | | 2 | 3 | | 4 |

| With a knickknack | paddywack | give the dog a bone |  |
|---|---|---|---|
| ♩ | ♩ | ♩ | ♩ |
| 1 | 2 | 3 | 4 |

| This | old | man | came | rolling | home |
|---|---|---|---|---|---|
| ♩ | | ♩ | | ♩ | ♩ |
| 1 | | 2 | | 3 | 4 |

| This | old | man | he | plays | two |
|---|---|---|---|---|---|
| ♩ | | ♩ | ♩ | | ♩ |
| 1 | | 2 | 3 | | 4 |

| He | plays | knickknack | on | my | shoe |
|---|---|---|---|---|---|
| ♩ | | ♩ | ♩ | | ♩ |
| 1 | | 2 | 3 | | 4 |

| With a knickknack | paddywack | give the dog a bone |  |
|---|---|---|---|
| ♩ | ♩ | ♩ | ♩ |
| 1 | 2 | 3 | 4 |

| This | old | man | came | rolling | home |
|---|---|---|---|---|---|
| ♩ | | ♩ | | ♩ | ♩ |
| 1 | | 2 | | 3 | 4 |

## Down In The Valley

| | | |
|---|---|---|
| Down ♩ 1 | in ♩ 2 | the ♩ 3 |
| val ♩ 1 | ♩ 2 | ley ♩ 3 |
| Val ♩ 1 | ley ♩ 2 | so ♩ 3 |
| low ♩ 1 | ♩ 2 | ♩ 3 |
| Hang ♩ 1 | your ♩ 2 | head ♩ 3 |
| o ♩ 1 | ♩ 2 | ver ♩ 3 |
| Hear ♩ 1 | the ♩ 2 | wind ♩ 3 |
| blow ♩ 1 | ♩ 2 | ♩ 3 |
| Hear ♩ 1 | the ♩ 2 | wind ♩ 3 |
| blow ♩ 1 | ♩ 2 | dear ♩ 3 |
| Hear ♩ 1 | the ♩ 2 | wind ♩ 3 |
| blow ♩ 1 | ♩ 2 | ♩ 3 |
| Hang ♩ 1 | your ♩ 2 | head ♩ 3 |
| o ♩ 1 | ♩ 2 | ver ♩ 3 |
| Hear ♩ 1 | the ♩ 2 | wind ♩ 3 |
| blow ♩ 1 | ♩ 2 | ♩ 3 |

with 4 beats to a measure. The music familiar to children is usually repetitious, and movement patterns or sequences can be repeated, matching movement phrases to music phrases. The two choruses of "This Old Man" don't have to be choreographically different. To accent the different words, make two separate moves, one for the words "one" and "thumb" in the first chorus and another for the words "two" and "shoe" in the second chorus.

## Grouping Measures

Once you are comfortable with counting beats and identifying measures, you're ready to group the measures into the musical phrasing. One way to clarify this method of organizing music is to compare it with the structure of the English language. Just as words are used to make sentences, and sentences are grouped to make paragraphs, beats are used to make measures and measures are grouped into phrases.

To make visible the way a piece of music is organized, you can use a slash mark (/) to symbolize each measure of 4 beats (4/4 time). These measures will be grouped on a line to indicate the natural breaks in the musical phrasing, determined by the music, as opposed to verbal phrasing, which is determined by the thoughts expressed by the words. Examples 1 and 2 chart the musical phrasing by keeping the slash marks on a single line for each phrase (see pages 26-27). Once the music has been charted, each phrase may be addressed individually.

You can teach students these three methods of counting and organizing music. Ask students to bring in some of their favorite pieces of music, one of which is selected by the class. The class listens to the music and identifies the rhythmic pattern by clapping out the beat. Using a chalkboard or drawing paper, make a chart following the examples mentioned. Now begin the process of choreography. Again, address one phrase at a time to simplify the task. To enhance their enthusiasm for dance, have the students bring in popular music to be used for choreography. This music tends to be easy to work with because it is thematic and repetitious, with phrasing that follows definite patterns. However, because of copyright laws, we can't use an illustrated charting of an existing recording. Therefore, example 3 (see page 28) is a format that is similar in pattern to most of today's popular music. Some choreographers organize their music in groups of 8 counts. This means that they use 2 measures of 4 counts (4/4 time) to equal one slash mark, which reflects 8 counts. The chart in example 3 uses this method.

### Three Blind Mice

| Lyrics/Phrases | "/" = 4 ♩ (beats) |
|---|---|
| Three blind mice, three blind mice | / / |
| See how they run, see how they run | / / |
| They all ran after the farmer's wife | / / / |
| She cut off their tails with a carving knife | |
| Did you ever see such a sight in your life | |
| As three blind mice | / |

Your chart should look like this:

| Phrase 1 | / / | total of 8 counts (or two 4s) |
|---|---|---|
| Phrase 2 | / / | total of 8 counts (or two 4s) |
| Phrase 3 | / / / | total of 12 counts (or three 4s) |
| Phrase 4 | / | total of 4 counts |

**This Old Man**

| Lyrics/Phrases | "/" = 4 ♩ (beats) |
|---|---|
| This old man, he plays one | / / |
| He plays knickknack on my thumb | |
| With a knickknack paddywack | / / |
| give the dog a bone | |
| This old man came rolling home | |
| This old man, he plays two | / / |
| He plays knickknack on my shoe | |
| With a knickknack paddywack | / / |
| give the dog a bone | |
| This old man came rolling home | |

Your chart should look like this:

| Phrase 1 | / / | total of 8 counts (or two 4s) |
|---|---|---|
| Phrase 2 | / / | total of 8 counts (or two 4s) |
| Phrase 3 | / / | total of 8 counts (or two 4s) |
| Phrase 4 | / / | total of 8 counts (or two 4s) |

## Grouping Measures Example 3

**Similar Pattern to Most of Today's Popular Songs**

Slash (/) equals eight counts

| | |
|---|---|
| Introduction | / / / / |
| Theme A | / / / |
| | / / |
| Theme B | / / / / |
| Transition | / / |
| Chorus | / / / / |
| Theme A | / / / |
| | / / |
| Theme B | / / / / |
| Transition | / / |
| Chorus | / / / / |
| Theme C | / / / / |
| | / / / / |
| | / / / / |
| Theme A | / / / |
| | / fades out |

# Summary

Understanding how movement skills and elements can be used for building dances gives you a basic knowledge of the origin of all movement. Also, understanding the social, cultural, and historical significance of dance gives you additional material to use when creating dances. Using music to frame a dance can be simple, once you learn how to organize and approach it.

# Chapter 3

# Constructing the Frame and Roof: Meaningful Organization of Materials

In this chapter you will find the tools to answer the following questions:

- How do you give dances structure?
- How can you dance a story?
- How can you use sounds, music, props, costume, and scenery?
- How can you put together a full production?

Now that you've assembled the materials to compose dances, it's time to get down to the nuts and bolts of organizing those materials. This chapter guides you through ways to structure dances use dance to portray a story line, use sound and props, and produce a performance.

# Structure and Choreographic Forms

You can structure dances in several ways. Often they are structured by music, and many terms in dance are taken from music terminology. Whether or not music is actually used, however, is irrelevant to the structuring of choreographic forms.

Four of the most popularly used choreographic forms are canon (also known as round), ABA, rondo, and theme and variation.

## Canon

Using a canon is like singing "Row, Row, Row Your Boat" in parts but using movement in place of or along with lyrics. This structure works well with younger as well as older children because of the small amount of material to remember and the familiarity of this musical pattern. Also, a little choreography goes a long way; that is, one movement pattern is repeated continuously.

### Movement Example

The class will learn the following 12-count (beat) combination, which is divided into three 4-count phrases.

(First phrase) Walk forward 4 steps (count 1, 2, 3, 4).

(Second phrase) Walk backward 4 steps (count 1, 2, 3, 4).

(Third phrase) Squat down (count 1), hold (count 2), stand (count 3), clap (count 4).

Next, divide the class into three groups and arrange them in a scattered formation across the room. Group 1 is on the right, group 2 is at center, and group 3 is on the left.

- Group 1 begins the first 4 counts while groups 2 and 3 remain motionless.

- As group 1 starts the second 4 counts, group 2 begins the first 4. Group 3 is still motionless.

- As group 1 starts the third 4 counts, group 2 begins the second 4, and group 3 begins the first 4.

- Each group stops after completing the entire 12-count combination three times in a row (36 counts in all). As groups finish, they should remain motionless until all groups have completed their 36 counts.

## Adding Variety to a Canon

Notice how the dances change when you modify them in some of the following ways:

- Use two groups instead of three.
- Begin the canon with group 1 on the left, 2 in the center, and 3 on the right.
- Arrange the groups from front to back with group 1 across the front, group 2 across the middle, and group 3 across the back.
- Reverse and begin back to front.
- Mix students from groups 1, 2, and 3 so that they are not standing next to anyone from their own group. Begin the canon with the students of group 1, then 2, then 3, making sure that the students are aware of their personal space and spatial relationships because they will be moving forward, backward, and up and down at the same time, while working next to each other.
- Start the combination with all groups moving in unison for all 36 counts. Repeat the combination in canon. When all groups have completed their 36 counts, the entire class repeats the combination in unison.

# ABA

The ABA form includes a movement phrase (A), a new movement phrase (B), and a return to the first movement phrase (A). You can help students understand this form by comparing it to a sandwich. The first layer is the bread (A), the peanut butter is the second (B), and another piece of bread is the third layer (A).

## Movement Example

Ask your students to do the following movements:

(A) Run across the floor, rotate two times, and then look at the audience.

(B) Kneel slowly, looking down at the floor and searching for something, then rise up quickly.

(A) Run across the floor, rotate two times, and then look at the audience.

### Adding Variety to ABA

- Class performs in unison.
- Divide class into two groups. One group does the A movement pattern each time it happens, and the other group does the B movement pattern.
- Divide class into three groups. One group does the first A, one group does the B, and a third group does the second A.

## Rondo

A rondo can be described as ABACADA. The choreographic pattern is A (the primary movement pattern), alternating with B, C, and D, which are different from A. To continue the imagery that we used with ABA, you can liken this form to a "super club sandwich."

### Movement Example

(A) Arms overhead, out to sides, in to waist, and down.

(B) March in place.

(A) Arms overhead, out to sides, in to waist, and down.

(C) Four quick leaps across the floor.

(A) Arms overhead, out to sides, in to waist, and down.

(D) Run in a circle.

(A) Arms overhead, out to sides, in to waist, and down.

### Adding Variety to Rondo

- One group of students performs A and freezes while other students perform B, C, and D.
- Students perform with their backs to the audience.
- Students can create a shorter dance by performing ABACA.

## Theme and Variation

The theme and variation form is a movement pattern with subsequent variations of the original pattern: A, A1, A2, A3.

### Movement Example

(A) Walk forward 8 steps.

(A1) Walk forward 8 steps while waving arms above head.

(A2) Walk forward 8 steps while clapping hands.

(A3) Walk forward 8 steps while bent over.

## Adding Variety to Theme and Variation
- One group of students performs the theme while at the same time a second group performs a variation of the theme.
- Students face different directions and perform the theme and variations in unison.
- Students perform the theme, then the first variation (A1). They then perform the theme, the first variation (A1), and then second variation (A2). They then perform the theme, the first variation (A1), the second variation (A2), and then the third variation (A3), and so on.

# Characterization and Story Line

Characterization is the backbone of dances that have a story line and of dances that show people interacting. Whenever a choreographer has to tell a story or bring a character to life, the image portrayed is an interpretation of the choreographer's perspective. This interpretation can be literal or abstract. Students can use brainstorming techniques to develop the qualities of a character and the movements that might show these qualities. When a choreographer chooses a few of these movements and repeats them every time that particular character appears, it will help the audience recognize "who" is dancing. This is called a movement signature.

### Movement Example
Start with the following story line:
Goldilocks encounters the three bears and is frightened.

- In a literal interpretation, dancers would explore movements that they think best express Goldilocks' actual reactions. (She could put her hands on her cheeks and pull back as if holding her breath.)
- In an abstract interpretation, the action would be more metaphorical. For example, the dancers might express a quality of fear. (She could skip around and then suddenly freeze, staring off into space.)

You can also base story lines on an actual piece of literature, a student-developed original story, or a collaborative effort between students and teacher. The story line can be the basis of one dance or an entire show, and you can use music and narration to enhance the story or make it easier to interpret.

Remember, a story dance, as in literature, should have a beginning, a middle, and an end. Consider the way events line up to present conflict, climax, and resolution. You could make a diagram to help you and the students design the order and subject matter of the dance sections. For instance, in the story of Goldilocks and the Three Bears, the event of Goldilocks exploring the three bears' cabin and falling asleep and the event of the three bears returning home to discover that someone else had been there both build up to the climax of the discovery of Goldilocks in the bed. The resolution of the story is when she runs out of the cabin, never to return.

See figure 3.1 for the high points and leveling of story line.

## Sounds and Music

Responding to sounds adds depth and dimension to choreography. Instead of using recorded music, you can have a class make their own sound score by using assorted rhythm instruments, homemade instruments, percussive clapping, slapping and snapping of various parts of the body, or vocal noises. The dancers or a different set of classmates can perform the "music" as accompaniment to the dancers.

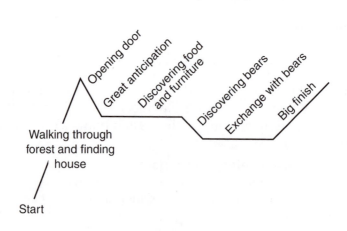

**FIGURE 3.1**   Story line diagram for Goldilocks and the Three Bears.

## Movement Examples

- Use the sounds of tearing paper, a bicycle horn, and a slide whistle. For each sound, create a movement and perform it to that sound.

- As students are walking, have them freeze in a pose on a single clap, change direction on the sound of a finger snap, and continue walking on a double clap.

In theater, another meaning for the term *sound* is what the audience hears and how recorded music can be amplified to create the best auditory experience. Depending on the equipment available to you, you can regulate the sound level so that the audience does not have to strain to hear, is not bothered by hums and whistles from the speakers, or is not blasted out of the performance space by disturbingly loud levels of music or a narrator's voice. In a large performance space you have to consider the dancers too. Make sure that a speaker is on stage so that the dancers can hear the music clearly. Their cues depend on it! In a really huge space you might think about a speaker in the backstage area so that the waiting dancers can also hear the music or narration.

# Props

The theatrical term *props* comes from the word *properties.* Actors would use a glass, flower, book, chair, hat, cane, and whatever else their imagination suggests. Dancers can also use props to add interest and different qualities to dance movement. For example, the hats that the dancers use in the finale of *A Chorus Line* add emphasis and establish a distinctive style to the choreography (figure 3.2). Developing movements, attitudes, and characters through the use of props can be a fun and interesting exercise.

## Movement Examples

- Have all students create a dance about rowing oars, incorporating the use of the oars in the actual movement.

- Have students create a dance about the yellow brick road from *The Wizard of Oz* by wearing tissue boxes painted yellow on their heads (figure 3.3).

**FIGURE 3.2** Simply adding hats conveys the excitement of Broadway.

**FIGURE 3.3** Using inexpensive props can easily portray an idea.

# Costumes

Costumes are an easy and effective way to enhance the meaning of the dance. They need not be expensive or elaborate. They just need to be appropriate for the ideas in a dance. To continue with our example of Goldilocks and the Three Bears, the three bears can wear brown sweatshirts and pants and paper masks. In addition, Mama Bear can wear an apron, Papa Bear can wear a vest, and Baby Bear can wear a bonnet or cap. Goldilocks can be dressed in any little-girl-type dress with a bow in her hair.

# Set Pieces and Scenery

There is a difference between the terms *scenery* and *set pieces*. Set pieces are isolated pieces of stage décor or decorations. Set pieces can be very inexpensive to make and are easily moved on and off the stage area. They can be made out of ply-score cardboard, which is corrugated cardboard with four or more layers, and backed with strips of lumber. Some examples of set pieces are a bush, trees, a doorframe, a window frame, and fences. Other examples of set pieces that do not have to be constructed are furniture, a trunk (luggage), benches, standing mirrors, and a coat tree. The difference between a prop and a set piece is that a prop is usually carried and used by a performer, and a set piece is usually stationary once it is placed.

Scenery is a completely different concept. It could consist of a painted backdrop that is rented. A backdrop decorates the very back of the stage area. If you were performing *A Midsummer's Night Dream*, your backdrop would be painted to look like a forest. You can make your own backdrop with help from the visually creative people in your school. You can make it out of canvas that covers the back wall of the stage area, and you can hang it from the battens (pipes). You should paint it while it's flat on the floor and hang it when it is dry. An easier, less expensive alternative is to measure out sheets of brown paper on which you paint your scene. You would then attach the paper to the back wall of the stage area. Glue, tape, or staples will do the job depending on the nature of the back wall.

If you have the resources of an industrial arts program, a technical theater program, or an art department, you can combine your energies to make a spectacular-looking set. Scenery will add a whole new look to your production.

# Full Production

There are many rewards to planning and staging a full production. More of the students' work will be showcased. The performers will gain pride and self-esteem from a job well done. You will create public awareness and support for your program, and the school environment will be energized by the enthusiasm and creativity of the students. Be sure to enlist all the help you can. Fellow faculty members, members of the community (both arts and cultural), and parents of your students can be excellent resources for enhancing your project and bringing the whole production to a high educational and entertainment level.

"Backward planning" is a tool that you can use for planning a production. Start by imagining what the final production should contain. Divide the performing responsibilities among classes or groups of students. If you are following a story line, you need to think about how each of the dances moves the story line forward. In a full production, you should consider sound, props, costumes, and perhaps scenery and set pieces for each section of your production. With these goals in mind, start the work.

# Summary

Knowledge of choreographic forms is necessary when you're assembling material into a dance. These forms provide a structure for the material. Choreographic forms include the canon (or round), ABA, rondo, and theme and variation. You and your students can explore each form and discover countless possibilities for structuring movement.

The use of characterization is essential to dances with a story line. Students can use brainstorming techniques to develop movements that portray characters. The interpretation can be literal or abstract. The use of sounds, props, costumes, set pieces, and scenery will add further dimensions to your choreographic endeavors, taking an idea into a full production.

# Chapter 4

# Adding Architectural Details: Customizing Dances

In this chapter you will find the tools to answer the following questions:

- What is accenting?
- How can you use gestures?
- What is stylizing and how do you use it?
- How do you use expressive quality to enhance a dance?

Certain details of dance can enhance creativity and help you deliver the choreographic message to the audience. Consider using the following when choreographing: accents, gestures, stylizing, and expressive qualities.

# Accents: Adding Emphasis

You can choreograph in the same way that you accent music. Accenting choreography makes a section of a movement pattern stronger, adds interest, and highlights a particular moment in the music. An accent occurs when a move is made bolder, when the surprise of a sharp move is interjected in a slow section, or when a position is held for a longer time.

Additionally, accenting (making stronger) a different beat in each measure adds variety. Have the students stamp on the bold numbers in the following 16-count walking activity.

First measure **1** 2 3 4

Second measure 1 **2** 3 4

Third measure 1 2 **3** 4

Fourth measure 1 2 3 **4**

Students can play around with this concept by clapping as well as walking. Some could clap as an accompaniment as others walk. At times, only the accented beat needs to be clapped. Following is an extended example of the walking and clapping dance phrase.

Students create a 4-count walking movement pattern. They may or may not wish to change direction with each measure. As a group or as individuals, with you as the director, they develop a large locomotor or nonlocomotor movement to do on the accented count. This might take the form of a jump, leap, kneel, twist, or arm thrust. The complete dance phrase might look like this:

First measure: **leap 1,** walk 2, walk 3, walk 4

Second measure: walk 1, **twist 2,** walk 3, walk 4

Third measure: walk 1, walk 2, **jump 3,** walk 4

Fourth measure: walk 1, walk 2, walk 3, **kneel 4**

Students can reorder the measures so that the accents appear to be mixed up. They could memorize the patterns and make the dance phrase longer by adding the mixed-up versions.

# Gestures: Telling the Story Through Movement

Gestures are valuable tools in getting a message across from the dancers to the audience. They include movements of the body, head, arms, hands, or face that express an idea, opinion, or emotion. Gestures, for example, are an important component of many folk and ethnic dance forms. The art of pantomime uses gestures exclusively, going from one gesture to the next to tell a story or portray a thought. An example is a simple gesture we all use: a wave. A wave can be performed to mean any of the following:

Hello

Good-bye

Come here

Go away

Stop

Go

Can I have your attention?

Divide your students into small groups. Have each group choose three different waves. The students then create dance phrases using all three of these waves. As a final step in the activity, have the dance phrases of the individual small groups connect to the other small-group phrases, thereby creating a "paragraph" of movement.

# Stylizing: Creating a Place and Time

There is a difference between style and stylizing. For example, the names of choreographers or famous dancers bring a particular style to mind. In ballet, it is George Balanchine and Enrico Cecchetti; in modern dance, Martha Graham and Merce Cunningham; in tap, Fred Astaire, Savion Glover (the Tap Dance Kid), and Gregory Hines; and in jazz, Bob Fosse. Gene Kelly had a style of his own that combined ballet with Broadway. One such example is his work *An American in Paris* set to George Gershwin's musical score. It is part of the film *An American in Paris,* in which he stars, but the dance piece is now available as a separate video.

The term *stylized,* however, refers to a dance done with the flavor of a country, a vernacular dance (dance from a specific social era, such as the Charleston, minuet, cabbage patch, or break dance), or one of the formal dance disciplines. After watching selected videos or films, viewing live performances, or looking at pictures in dance publications, students should be able to see the differences between a style of dancing and the stylizing of a piece of choreography to fit a time and place.

The following examples illustrate the meaning of *stylized*. Your students, with or without your input, make a dance phrase. They stand in a line across the front of the performance space. Their feet are slightly apart and their arms are extended in the air to form a V.

From this position they jump forward twice.

They do a jump with a half turn and face the back.

They continue the rotation and finish facing the way they started.

What could they do to make this simple phrase look like a cave painting?

- They could bend their elbows to make a square shape.
- They could keep their heads turned to the right.
- They could bend their knees and keep them apart.

What could they do to make this simple phrase look like the Rockettes from Radio City Music Hall?

- They could spread their fingers apart with high energy.
- They could do a step–kick going forward instead of doing a jump.
- They could spin the half turn instead of jumping.

These two opposite ends of the time and place spectrum give you an indication of what to look for and what to add when you want to make a piece of choreography look different. A dance doesn't have to be technically or traditionally correct or historically accurate (figure 4.1). What's important is the impression it gives the audience. Another example of stylization is the dance sequence "America" from *West Side Story,* in which the dancers don't actually do the dances of Puerto Rico but give an impression of that country with a turn of the wrist and a flick of the hip. They also respond to the cultural flavor of the music. People develop their own style, a signature, with identifiable features. Students who use their styles but not the actual steps of the dance are said to be stylizing.

**Figure 4.1**   Choreography need not be authentic to give the impression of time and place.

## Expressive Qualities: Creating Moods Through Movement

Expressive qualities, or moods, are important in choreography, especially in dances that have a theme or story line. The mood or expressive quality can affect the *what*, the *how*, and the *why* of a dance. If an emotional quality is used at the beginning of the dance-making process, it affects the type of movement chosen, thereby shaping the actual structure, steps, and dance phrases—the *what* of a dance composition. Expressive qualities can refer to *how* a movement is done. How a movement is done focuses the dancer and the audience on the intention of the movement, or *why* the movement is being done. For example, if the teacher asks students to make up a dance phrase that communicates the idea of an angry young child, students may choose to use stomping walks and falls to the floor to represent a temper tantrum. The students choose the *what,* or the movement skills, based on the word *angry*. Still motivated by the mood *angry*, the students perform the movements with great strength and percussive energy. *How* the movement is done represents the word *angry*. The intent, or *why* the movement is being done, is to remind the audience of what some young children do when they do not get their own way.

Changes in facial expressions enhance the performance of gestures and movement, but that is only part of the picture. Expressive

**FIGURE 4.2** When a dancer is slumped and looking at the floor, the audience will feel the loss.

qualities are displayed in the body posture. For example, as in figure 4.2, a body slumped over shows fatigue, sadness, or dejection. Contrasting this image, a body sitting very tall and erect shows alertness or happiness. The amount of energy used will also be controlled by the mood to be expressed. If students are to move as though they are in a peaceful mood, they will use smooth and gentle energy. If they are to move as though they are in an excited mood, they will employ erratic, quick energy.

As a side benefit, dance allows students to express their emotions in a nonthreatening and accepting atmosphere. By exploring various moods and emotions through movement, students can even experience a level of emotional release and learn to interact with each other in an appropriate manner.

Here is a simple dance activity that enhances students' abilities to express mood:

1. To get everyone's creative juices flowing, brainstorm various moods and emotions.
2. Have the class spread out across the space.

3. Tell them that you will call out a mood or emotion from the brainstorm list, and they are to immediately do movements (staying relatively in place) that express this mood or emotion.

4. Remind the students that they are communicating through movement, so sounds and talking are not necessary. They should try to be as expressive as possible with their movements.

# Summary

Adding the finishing touches to dances can make the difference between a series of movements that are merely joined together and a well-rounded dance piece that makes a personal statement. The effective use of accents, gestures, stylizing, and expressive qualities can provide those finishing touches.

# Chapter 5

# Putting It All Together: The Choreographic Process

In this chapter you will find the tools to answer the following questions:

- How do you choose subject matter?
- How can you explore and select movements?
- How can you coordinate music and movements?
- How can you further explore possibilities?
- When do you refine and memorize choreography?
- When can you add finishing touches?
- When is it time to perform choreography?

Just follow these seven easy steps, and voilà—you and your students will have a completed dance. You can also ask them to keep a journal as they work on the creative or dance-making process. Just ask the students to reflect and write on what they did to complete each of the seven steps. A journal prompt appears after each section. Journal writing is a good tool to make students' learning visible. Journal entries for each step are provided at the end of the chapter.

## Step 1: Choose Subject Matter

Students can choose their own story line, theme, or topic; or they may choose to use any of the "blueprints" for building dances, found in chapter 7. Use journal entry 1 with this step.

## Step 2: Explore and Select Movements

The next step is to explore movements based on the subject matter through a creative process (brainstorming and improvising) or by combining basic movement and dance skills. Students can use the Deal a Dance cards in two ways to find and select movements and dance skills that are appropriate to the subject matter. In the first way, they can randomly choose Sports and Game Movements (blue) cards or Dance Technique (orange) cards to make dance phrases. Using the appropriate Elements That Change Movements (green) cards, they then change how the movements are done so that the dance phrases fit the subject matter. The second way of using the Deal a Dance cards is to first look through all the cards to choose movements and qualities. Next use the Creative Movement Suggestions (purple) cards that you think are the most appropriate for the subject matter. You or your students, depending on their ages and abilities, can make these choices. Use journal entry 2 with this step.

## Step 3: Coordinate Music and Movements

If you're using music, organize it by using the counting of beats or verbal phrasing, as described in chapter 2 in "Organizing Music" (page 20). You can put combinations of movements to the musical or verbal phrases. Following are examples using "This Old Man" and "Rock-a-Bye Baby" (see page 49) or almost any popular song (see page 50). When choreographing, use a combination of counting beats and verbal phrasing. Verbal phrasing allows you to emphasize a particular word or phrase within the music.

When you add music to the creative process of building a dance, you add a medium that can be likened to the mortar that holds the layers of bricks together. Music supports and beautifies the elements of dance and adds interest. Use journal entry 3 with this step.

## This Old Man

| Phrase | Choreography |
|--------|--------------|
| 1 | Step, hop, step, hop (beats 1, 2, 3, 4) |
|   | Step, 2 claps, hold (beats 1, 2, 3, 4) |
| 2 | Step, kick, step, kick (beats 1, 2, 3, 4) |
|   | Step, kick, stamp, hold (beats 1, 2, 3, 4) |
| 3 | Spin on one foot (beats 1, 2), two jumps (3, 4) |
|   | Four claps on thighs (beats 1, 2, 3, 4) |
| 4 | Four runs (beats 1, 2, 3, 4) |
|   | Three runs (beats 1, 2, 3), kneel on one knee with arms reaching out (beat 4) |

## Rock-a-Bye Baby

**Section 1 Choreography**
*Rock-a-bye baby*
Cradle arms while swinging them to right and left.

**Section 2 Choreography**
*on the tree top*
Turn and face the back with arms lifted and fingers spread out.

**Section 3 Choreography**
*When the wind blows*
Sway body right and left in the same position.

**Section 4 Choreography**
*the cradle will rock*
Turn to front with arms in cradle position and sway right and left.

**Section 5 Choreography**
*When the bough breaks*
Reach out and clap hands on word *breaks*.

**Section 6 Choreography**
*the cradle will fall*
Body "melts" down; end sitting on floor.

**Section 7 Choreography**
*and down will come baby, cradle and all!*
Reach arms up to "catch" baby and pull arms into lap.

## Almost Any Popular Song in 4/4 Time

| Phrase | Choreography |
|---|---|
| Introduction | Dancers begin in a scattered formation. |
| 1-4 | 1. (First 8) Stand straddle, hands on shoulders; hold 8 counts. |
| | 2. (Second 8) Squat down, with head down, hands on floor; hold 8 counts. |
| | 3. (Third 8) Look at audience; hold 8 counts. |
| | 4. (Fourth 8) Slowly rise up, in 7 counts; strike any pose on count 8. |
| Theme A | |
| 1-3 | 1. Walk 3 steps forward; clap on count 4; walk 3 backward; clap on count 8. |
| | 2. Walk to the side, 3 steps to the right; clap on count 4; reverse. |
| | 3. Make four poses; hold each pose for 2 counts. |
| 4-5 | 4-5. Walk for 16 counts, around and through neighbors in a scattered formation (like a busy street scene). |
| Theme B | |
| 1-4 | Repeat the introduction. |
| Transition | |
| 1-2 | 1-2. Take 16 counts to form two concentric circles. |
| Chorus | |
| 1-4 | 1. Inside circle jogs clockwise 8 counts; outside circle jogs counterclockwise 8 counts. |
| | 2. Reverse. |
| | 3. Take 4 counts; all converge to center forming one large cluster; all face audience on counts 5-8. |
| | 4. Use 8 counts to jog back to original scattered formation. |
| Theme A | |
| 1-5 | Repeat theme A. |
| Theme B | |
| 1-4 | Repeat theme B. |
| Transition | |
| 1-2 | Repeat transition. |
| Chorus | |
| 1-2 | Repeat chorus. |

Theme C

| | |
|---|---|
| 1-12 | 1-11. Repeat the first three 8s of theme A as a three-part canon. |
| | 12. Walk around and through neighbors in a scattered formation for 8 counts. |

Theme A

| | |
|---|---|
| 1-3 | Repeat theme A. |
| 4-5 | Walk scattered and leave the stage as the music fades. |

# Step 4: Explore Possibilities

You can alter and enhance choreography by using changes and variations of level, focus, direction, rhythm, floor pattern, and placement of dancers. (Level, focus, direction, and floor patterns are addressed in chapter 2 under "Movement Elements.") You can alter a single movement or an entire movement pattern by changing any of the movement elements. Use journal entry 4 with this step.

## Rhythm Changes

Change of rhythm results from varying the way you use counts. Look at how many ways you can change a simple walking pattern. The walks in each of the following 4-beat measures are changed as indicated.

- Take four steps (one movement per beat).

  | step | step | step | step |
  |---|---|---|---|
  | 1 (♩) | 2 (♩) | 3 (♩) | 4 (♩) |

- Take two steps (holding 1 beat after each step).

  | step | hold | step | hold |
  |---|---|---|---|
  | 1 (♩) | 2 (♩) | 3 (♩) | 4 (♩) |

- Take one step (hold for 3 additional beats).

  | step | hold | hold | hold |
  |---|---|---|---|
  | 1 (♩) | 2 (♩) | 3 (♩) | 4 (♩) |

- Take five steps (first three on beats 1, &, 2, the next two on beats 3, 4)

  | step | step | step | step | step |
  |---|---|---|---|---|
  | 1 (♩) | & (♪) 2 (♩) | | 3 (♩) | 4 (♩) |

- Take eight steps (1 & 2 & 3 & 4 &). This pattern is called double time.

| step | step | step | step | step | step | step | step |
|------|------|------|------|------|------|------|------|
| 1 (♪) | & (♪) | 2 (♪) | & (♪) | 3 (♪) | & (♪) | 4 (♪) | & (♪) |

## Direction and Formation Changes

Stage directions (figure 5.1) are important because they establish common reference points. Students in all age groups should learn the stage directions in order to understand and use directional instructions. Choreographers and teachers use stage directions to tell the dancers which direction to face and in which direction to travel.

The use of different formations can frame, highlight, and add interest to the choreography. Formation refers to the placement of dancers on the stage.

Figure 5.2 shows sample formations that you can use to group dancers. Dancers can be stationary or moving while in these formations, and they may change formations many times during a dance. Groups of formations can perform individually or in unison. A layering of movements within the formations creates an additional effect.

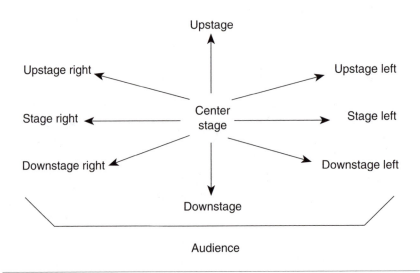

**FIGURE 5.1**  Stage directions.

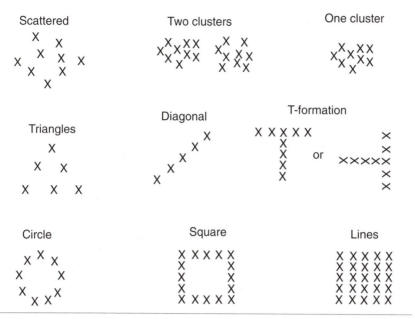

**Scattered**

```
     X   X
   X   X   X
 X   X   X   X
   X   X
     X
```

**Two clusters**

```
 X X XX    X   X
X X XX    X X X
   X       X X
         X  X X
```

**One cluster**

```
 X X XX
X X XX
   X
```

**Triangles**

```
     X
   X   X
 X   X   X
```

**Diagonal**

```
         X
       X
     X
   X
 X
```

**T-formation**

```
X X X X X        X
    X            X
    X    or  × × × × ×
    X            X
    X            X
```

**Circle**

```
   X X X
  X     X
 X       X
  X X X
```

**Square**

```
X X X X X
X       X
X       X
X       X
X X X X X
```

**Lines**

```
X X X X X
X X X X X
X X X X X
X X X X X
X X X X X
```

**FIGURE 5.2**  Sample formations.

## Formation Example 1

While in a scattered formation, the front half of the group kneels and waves their hands while the back half stands and steps side to side (figure 5.3).

**FIGURE 5.3**  Layering movements can create an additional effect.

### Formation Example 2

The group condenses to a huddle as in football, with bodies hunched together in a tight circle. They may have arms around each other or pulled into their centers (figure 5.4).

**Figure 5.4**  A football huddle formation shows unity.

### Formation Example 3

Experiment with a pyramid, as used in cheerleading. Divide the group so that the most people and strongest people are at the base. People can be standing or on their hands and knees. The next group of fewer people get onto the shoulders or the backs of the base people. End with one person on top (figure 5.5).

# Step 5: Refine and Memorize Choreography

Make sure that all dancers perform the movement sequences as choreographed, and make corrections before the errors become learned behavior. You and your students may want to show the dance to an outside viewer or videotape a rehearsal in order to help you make improvements in the performance. (See chapter 6 for more information on using video for evaluating and revising your dance.) Once the dance is "cleaned up," rehearse it, rehearse it, and rehearse it again. The body must learn the dance so that if stage fright occurs, muscle memory will take over. Use journal entry 5 with this step.

**FIGURE 5.5**   A pyramid formation shows strength and balance.

## Step 6: Add Finishing Touches

Performing a dance is more than just walking through the choreography. Dancers shouldn't hold back; they should perform the choreography full out. They need to smile, acknowledge the audience, use appropriate amounts and types of energy, and execute every movement to its fullest—in other words, have stage presence. Costumes can range from simple to elaborate depending on budget and availability. Whether the costumes are street clothing, a simple T-shirt, or an elaborate outfit ordered from a catalog, they make the dance special and thus make the students feel special. No matter how simple or inexpensive, costumes should be a part of every performance.

Lighting and scenery are a wonderful addition to any performance, but they're not always necessary or available. Set pieces can be a collaborative effort with the visual arts department and are alternatives to a full set. If stage lighting is not available, a simple on-and-off to blackout will establish some desired effects. Use journal entry 6 with this step.

## Step 7: Perform the Choreography

Once you have refined and practiced the choreography and added the finishing touches, the piece is ready to be performed. Whether the performance is in an informal setting (such as a gymnasium or multipurpose room) or in a traditional auditorium with a stage, the students will revel in the thrill of performing. They can perform for their peers, for younger children, or for their parents and community members. Once the dancers have the confidence, and you are sure they are up to it, you can have them perform at community functions. If you have several classes in which you work out choreographic problems and build dances, you will have enough material to do a concert on your own, or you can collaborate with the music teacher or director to do a joint concert. Use journal entry 7 with this step.

# Summary

Creating a dance can be as simple as following the seven steps. By taking one step at a time, students can make the creative process far less intimidating or difficult. By building one dance at a time, you can reach the goal of constructing an entire dance concert.

Student's name:_____ Date: _____

1. The theme or idea for my dance is

2. I chose this theme or idea because

Student's name:_____ Date: _____

Write about the process that you used to explore and select movements for your dance.

1. How did you explore and choose the movements?

2. How did you select and organize these movements into dance phrases?

3. Did you use any of the dance structures such as canon, rondo, ABA, or others? Which ones?

From *Building Dances, Second Edition,* by Susan McGreevy-Nichols, Helene Scheff, and Marty Sprague, 2005, Champaign, IL: Human Kinetics.

Student's name:_____ Date: _____

1. I chose _____ (music or sound selection) because

2. I chose to use verbal phrasing, counting of beats, or a combination of both methods (circle one). (Use the space below to show your work.)

From *Building Dances, Second Edition,* by Susan McGreevy-Nichols, Helene Scheff, and Marty Sprague, 2005, Champaign, IL: Human Kinetics.

Student's name:_____ Date: _____

1. Describe any rhythm changes that you used to make variations in your dance phrases or sections of the dance.

How did these changes vary the look or feeling of the dance phrases or sections?

2. Describe the stage directions you are using for facings and traveling directions.

3. If you are making a group dance, diagram your most important formations in the space below.

From *Building Dances, Second Edition,* by Susan McGreevy-Nichols, Helene Scheff, and Marty Sprague, 2005, Champaign, IL: Human Kinetics.

Student's name:_____ Date: _____

1. Using the Performance Assessment Checklist (provided by your teacher), evaluate the performance of your dance. If it is a solo, you will have to use videotape to evaluate your own performance or have a peer assess you. List here what you need to improve in the performance of your dance.

2. Using the Suggested Criteria (provided by your teacher) for a dance, evaluate your choreography and make any changes or revisions. List these changes here.

From *Building Dances, Second Edition,* by Susan McGreevy-Nichols, Helene Scheff, and Marty Sprague, 2005, Champaign, IL: Human Kinetics.

## Journal Entry 6

Student's name:_____ Date: _____

1. Sketch or describe your costumes.

2. Sketch or describe any scenery or props.

3. Describe lighting colors, brightness (levels), and when they should happen in the dance (cues).

Student's name:_____ Date: _____

1. Have audience members or peers use the Performance Critique (provided by your teacher) to evalaute your dance. Write the most interesting comments here. Make sure to list comments that are complimentary and comments that indicate ways in which your work could be made better.

2. Describe the most important thing you learned in completing this dance project. Explain why this learning was important to you.

From *Building Dances, Second Edition,* by Susan McGreevy-Nichols, Helene Scheff, and Marty Sprague, 2005, Champaign, IL: Human Kinetics.

# Chapter 6

# Inspecting Your Creation: Observation to Assessment

In this chapter you will find the tools to answer the following questions:

- How can student work be evaluated?
- What are outcomes, standards, criteria, and rubrics?
- How can you and your students evaluate a new dance?
- How can students judge other students' dances and performances?
- How can students critique professional performances?

Choreographers, like contractors, must inspect their products. When the dance is completed, the work must be judged as successful or in need of improvement. Evaluating dances and other student work is possible. Teachers, as well as students, can learn to observe, critique, revise, and evaluate dances. The key to assessment is to use it to improve everyone's current and future work.

# Student Assessment: Standards, Criteria, and Rubrics

Evaluating class work (activities, assignments, tasks, and projects) is a necessary part of the educational process. Evaluation should be used to make the students' work better. How do you evaluate students' work? You need standards and criteria. National standards exist so that all students can have the same opportunities to learn and can be held accountable for the same information. The National Dance Standards and the National Standards for Physical Education are outlined in the appendix, and they are listed for each activity in chapter 7.

Criteria are items that should be included in each student's work. Criteria can be taken from the particular skills or knowledge the students are working with, explanations of good work taken from the standards, and teachers' and students' requirements for the work. Evaluation can be formal or informal. Checklists are a simple listing of criteria that can be used as a guide in students' work. For example, in evaluating a student's movement skills, the teacher gives a student the Movement Skills Checklist (see page 70) before the student begins working, and the student uses it during the process so that she can demonstrate that she knows all the components of the work.

Rubrics place a value on the work. Teachers use rubrics as a guide in grading a project; rubrics also help the students to determine when their work is complete. The following is an example of a simple rubric.

3: Above standard. The work is complete. All the criteria are included, plus the student expands the work and demonstrates not only complete control of the idea or skills but also an understanding of the material at a higher level.

2: At standard. The work is complete. All the criteria are included; student demonstrates control of the idea or skills.

1: More work is needed. Part of the work is not done. More teaching may be required for understanding.

For example, in an assignment that asks students to create a dance phrase from the two Creative Movement Suggestions (purple) cards of rising and sinking, the following rubric could be used:

3: Above standard. The dance phrase includes an opening shape or entrance, is longer than 4 measures of 8 counts, explores the ideas of rising and sinking in the "Try This" suggestions, communicates a story or an action found in nature, and has an ending shape or an exit.

2: At standard. The dance phrase includes an opening shape or entrance, is at least 4 measures of 8 counts, explores the ideas of rising and sinking in the "Try This" suggestions, and has an ending shape or an exit.

1: More work is needed. The dance phrase is missing any of the criteria in the "at standard" level. More work or revision is needed.

Ideally, when planning a lesson or unit, you as the teacher first consider students' learning. What are the content knowledge and skills that the students should demonstrate control over? Then you should consider the assessment of the learning. What is the product that will prove that the students have learned the knowledge and skills? What are the criteria to be included in the assessment? Is a rubric needed or is a checklist or observation sufficient? Finally, you should plan the instruction and interim steps that will prepare students for their demonstration of knowledge and skills.

# Outcomes for Dance: Six Areas of Assessment

Outcomes are the desired results of any given lesson. Outcomes for dance can include six areas of assessment: movement skills, choreographic and creative process, cognitive skills, social skills, performance skills, and aesthetic skills. Following are criteria checklists, evaluations, rubrics, and observation checklists that can be used with the dance-building activities in chapter 7 or perhaps in your own lesson plans.

• **Movement skills.** Movement skills refer to a student's ability to develop a movement vocabulary composed of specific movement skills and movement elements. To evaluate the student's ability with movement skills and elements, use all or part of the Movement Skills Checklist (found at the end of the chapter).

• **Choreographic and creative process.** The choreographic and creative process refers to the student's ability to use movement skills and elements in order to improvise or create choreography. Before their dances are performed, most professional choreographers have trusted friends watch and critique their dances, or they have their dances videotaped so that they can decide on and make necessary changes. It is always good to learn from the pros. Before performing the new dance, have peers evaluate the dance by using the Criteria for a Dance Checklist (page 71); or have the dance videotaped and, after watching the tape, you and your students complete this checklist.

• **Cognitive skills.** Cognitive skills refer to a student's ability to solve problems and use critical-thinking skills and memorization skills as well as conceptualization, verbalization, and listening skills. To evaluate cognitive skills, use all or part of the Anecdotal Observation Checklist: Cognitive Skills (see page 72).

• **Social skills.** Social skills refer to the student's ability to work cooperatively and exhibit self-control. To evaluate a student's social skills, use the Social Skills Checklist (see page 73).

• **Performance skills.** A videotape of the performance of the dance can be a valuable tool for documenting and assessing students' work. Just as you can use the videotape to evaluate the dance itself, you can also use it to evaluate the students' performance of the dance. Use the Student's Performance Assessment Form (see page 74) after viewing a live performance or a videotape. This particular form was developed with input from students, who gave the criteria that they thought were important for a successful performance. You can adapt this form to any situation by adding your own or the students' criteria to make it relevant to the specific work and performance.

• **Aesthetic skills.** During a performance, the person viewing the dance piece can observe and assess individual dancers, individual pieces of choreography, and the performance as a whole (figure 6.1). The viewer can make observations about what they like or dislike about a performance or a dance. Have students watch live or videotaped concerts performed by other students and professionals. By critiquing professional performances, your students will be able to develop their own values, likes, and dislikes. With this information, students can then easily develop their own style of choreography. Students are capable of assessing their own, peers',

**Figure 6.1**   Viewing live performances is a vital part of the learning experience.

and professional dancers' performances; in the process, they develop their personal aesthetics. Note that you may need to caution students who have had limited experience critiquing. Remind them to keep their comments constructive. Use the forms titled Performance Critique for Grades K to 6 (page 75) and Performance Critique for Grades 7 to 12 (page 76) when assessing videotaped and live performances. The forms ask grade-appropriate questions for critiquing a performance.

## Summary

Student assessment is necessary for effective teaching and learning. In addition to evaluating students' learning of skills and concepts, you should evaluate cognitive and social skills gained during the activity. The checklists included in this chapter will help you and your students begin the process of effective evaluation.

Students need the opportunity to express how they feel about a piece of art, whether it is a work created and performed by professionals, by themselves, or by their peers. The performance assessment and critique forms can help facilitate this kind of personal expression.

## Movement Skills Checklist (Teacher or Peer)

Student's name:_____ Class: _____

Student demonstrates control of the following movement skills:

1. Locomotor movements (choose from the list of grade-appropriate movement skills in chapter 2, p. 15-16):

2. Nonlocomotor movements (choose from the list of grade-appropriate movement skills in chapter 2, p. 15-16):

Student can demonstrate control and understanding of the following movement elements:

1. Shape: ❏ curved  ❏ twisted  ❏ straight  ❏ angular  ❏ symmetrical ❏ asymmetrical
2. Space: ❏ direction  ❏ facing  ❏ size of movement/shape  ❏ levels ❏ floor patterns  ❏ focus
3. Time: ❏ tempo (speed)  ❏ moving to rhythms
4. Force: ❏ energy  ❏ quality  ❏ movement flow

From *Building Dances, Second Edition,* by Susan McGreevy-Nichols, Helene Scheff, and Marty Sprague, 2005, Champaign, IL: Human Kinetics.

## Criteria for a Dance Checklist

Student's name:_____ Class: _____

The dance has (pp. 11-12):    ___ A beginning

___ A middle

___ An end

Movement skills (pp. 14-16):    ___ Locomotor movements

___ Nonlocomotor movements

___ Body positions/shapes

Movement elements (p. 16):    ___ Shape

___ Space

___ Time

___ Force

Your dance has a theme or idea:    ___ Your own idea

___ Based on ethnic or cultural backgrounds (p. 16)

___ Based on historical or social dances (p. 17)

You have included choreographic forms (pp. 30-33):

___ Canon

___ ABA

___ Rondo

___ Story line

You have included appropriate ___ sounds or ___ music (p. 34).

You have included ___ props or ___ scenery (pp. 35-37).

You have included ___ accents, ___ gestures, ___ stylization, ___ expressive qualities (pp. 40-45).

You have included ___ rhythm changes, ___ formations, ___ different facings, ___ different traveling directions (pp. 51-54).

From *Building Dances, Second Edition,* by Susan McGreevy-Nichols, Helene Scheff, and Marty Sprague, 2005, Champaign, IL: Human Kinetics.

## Anecdotal Observation Checklist: Cognitive Skills

Student's name:_____ Class: _____

1. I have observed this student's ability to solve problems. He or she has created an acceptable movement or dance phrase according to the following prompt: _____

This student received _____ (grade), according to the following rubric: (write rubric in space below):

<br><br><br><br><br>

2. I have observed this student's ability to use critical thinking skills. He or she was able to compare, contrast, and choose the best solution or improvement for a dance phrase or dance.
   - ❏ chose the best solution/improvement, was able to defend the choice, and added more clarity and detail to the solution/improvement
   - ❏ chose the best solution and was able to defend the choice
   - ❏ demonstrated some trouble making a choice or could not defend the choice

3. I have observed this student's memorization skills. He or she was able to accurately demonstrate memorization of dance phrase(s)/dance(s).
   - ❏ All of the time without extra practice
   - ❏ All of the time with extra practice
   - ❏ Most of the time without extra practice
   - ❏ Most of the time with extra practice
   - ❏ Sometimes without extra practice
   - ❏ Sometimes with extra practice

4. I have observed this student's verbalization and listening skills. He or she was able to demonstrate the following:
   - ❏ Stays on topic during a conversation
   - ❏ Can bring up new topics
   - ❏ Can elaborate on answers
   - ❏ Asks appropriate questions
   - ❏ Can paraphrase another's questions or responses

From *Building Dances, Second Edition,* by Susan McGreevy-Nichols, Helene Scheff, and Marty Sprague, 2005, Champaign, IL: Human Kinetics.

## Social Skills Checklist (Teacher or Peer)

Student's name:_____ Class: _____

This student demonstrates the following social skills during activities that require teamwork:

_____ 1. Uses appropriate turn-taking behaviors.

_____ 2. Looks for other students' opinions or ideas.

_____ 3. Does not take over the conversation or the work.

_____ 4. Volunteers his or her ideas.

_____ 5. Can explain ideas, choices, and feelings while working.

_____ 6. Follows through on responsibilities.

_____ 7. Stays on task.

From *Building Dances, Second Edition,* by Susan McGreevy-Nichols, Helene Scheff, and Marty Sprague, 2005, Champaign, IL: Human Kinetics.

Name of student who is grading: _____

Name of student who is being graded:_____

**Instructions:** Grade each item on the form using a scale of 1 to 5 (1 being the least and 5 being the best).

### Scale: 1-5

5 = Always   4 = Most of the time   3 = Can improve   2 = Needs much improvement
1 = No attempt   NA = Not applicable   DK = Do not know

**Standards:** National Dance Standard 1, National Dance Standard 3 (see appendix)

Throughout the performance, the performer . . .

_____ 1. stayed in character.

_____ 2. showed energy.

_____ 3. looked at audience when appropriate.

_____ 4. smiled when appropriate.

_____ 5. covered up mistakes well.

_____ 6. reacted well to problems with lighting or music.

_____ 7. looked in the appropriate direction while dancing.

_____ 8. obeyed performance rules (did not touch costume, hair, or face; wear jewelry; and so on) while performing.

_____ 9. used proper facial expressions.

_____ 10. held endings.

_____ 11. acted seriously about the concert.

_____ 12. acted appropriately during performance (no talking, laughing, horsing around, touching others' props).

_____ 13. obeyed safety rules (no gum chewing, no touching backstage equipment).

_____ 14. remained calm before, during, and after performing.

_____ 15. was quiet in the wings.

_____ 16. made exits and entrances on time.

_____ 17. made movements full.

_____ 18. performed choreography as it was choreographed.

_____ 19. kept in time with the music.

_____ 20. executed the dance movements correctly.

_____ 21. reacted well to accents within the music.

_____ 22. was conscious of spacing concerns during the dance.

### Rubric

Above standard = 110-99 points   At standard = 98-77 points   Needs more work = 76-0 points

Name of student being graded: _____ Total score: _____

From *Building Dances, Second Edition,* by Susan McGreevy-Nichols, Helene Scheff, and Marty Sprague, 2005, Champaign, IL: Human Kinetics.

## Staging and choreography

1. Look for the area of the stage where most of the performance took place. Was it on the sides, in the middle, or close to the front or back?
2. Did the dancers use all of the floor space?
3. What dance movements did you recognize?
4. Describe your favorite movement.

## Costumes

1. Look for costumes that you like. Describe one.
2. What colors did you notice in the costumes? Why do you think the choreographer chose those colors?

## Lighting

1. What lighting changes did you notice?
2. Were the lights always white, or did they change color? What colors did you see?
3. Were there any special effects?

## Your feelings

1. Did the dancers look as if they knew what they were doing?
2. Was this a happy or sad dance? How could you tell?
3. Do you think any of the pieces were too long? Too short?
4. What piece did you like the best? Explain why.
5. What piece did you like the least? Explain why.

## Exercise

On a separate piece of paper, do the following:

1. Choose two pieces (or two dancers) and tell how they were alike or different.
2. With your class, discuss your own thoughts about the performance.

From *Building Dances, Second Edition,* by Susan McGreevy-Nichols, Helene Scheff, and Marty Sprague, 2005, Champaign, IL: Human Kinetics.

### Choreography and staging

1. Did the dancers use the whole stage or did they remain in one area of the stage?
2. What area of the stage seemed to catch your attention the most? Downstage? Stage left? Stage right? Upstage?
3. Did the movement change levels? Did the dancers go down to the floor? Were there any lifts?
4. Did the movement look difficult to do? Did the movement look simple? What made it look difficult or simple?
5. Describe your favorite movement.

### Music and sound score

1. Did the music or sound score enhance or detract from the choreography?
2. How well did the choreographer use the music? How well did the dancers use the music?

### Performance quality

1. What facial expressions did the dancers have? Did the facial expressions help you understand the piece?
2. Were the dancers focused on what they were doing?

### Costumes

1. Did the costumes catch your eye? Were they appropriate for the dance?
2. Did the costumes seem to restrict the dancers in their movement? Were the costumes easy to move in?

### Lighting

1. Was the stage well lit, or was it difficult to see the dancers?
2. Did the lighting change throughout the performance, or did it remain the same?
3. If you noticed changes in the lighting, what were they? How did the changes enhance the performance?

### Your observations

1. Did the performance seem too long? Too short?
2. What dance techniques did you recognize? Were they from ballet? Modern? Jazz? Other dance forms?
3. What was the audience' reaction?

4. What stood out most about the dancers? The choreography? The performance?
5. What dance or section of a dance did you like best? Explain why you made this choice.
6. What dance or section of a dance didn't you like? Explain why you made this choice.

## Exercise

On a separate piece of paper do the following:
1. Compare and contrast two pieces that you enjoyed the most.
2. In writing, discuss your own thoughts and feelings on the performance. Share your thoughts with others.

From *Building Dances, Second Edition,* by Susan McGreevy-Nichols, Helene Scheff, and Marty Sprague, 2005, Champaign, IL: Human Kinetics.

# Chapter 7

# Building Dances From Blueprints: Implementing the Choreographic Process

In this chapter you will find the tools to answer the following questions:

- What can I use as an inspiration?
- How can I make the materials accessible to students in different grades?
- How do I incorporate basic concepts and skills in dances?
- How can I apply criteria in assessing students?

The 15 dance-building activities in this chapter are designed for several purposes. Each is a fun learning experience using basic skills and concepts and is designed to be nonthreatening both to teachers and students. Each activity encourages some aspect of the creative process and makes the teacher a facilitator rather than a demonstrator.

Each dance activity has four sections: description of activity or procedure, sample activity, grade level suggestions, and criteria for assessment. These sections guide you through the activity to help you maximize its use. Communication with students is also a constant source of inspiration. Their willingness to cooperate and bring their thoughts and ideas to the class makes every day a rewarding and exciting experience.

# Deal a Dance

This activity fulfills the following standards:
   National Dance Standards: 1, 2, 3, 4, 7
   National Standards for Physical Education: 1, 2, 5, 6

This activity increases movement skills and movement vocabulary through the use of the enclosed 115 playing cards that are printed on both sides. Each card has two different movement skills or concepts for a total of 230 movement examples. Four types of cards facilitate the creation of movement patterns or pieces of choreography. This activity can be teacher facilitated, student directed, or both. You may use these cards for one class lesson or to build an entire unit.

## Description of Activity or Procedure

There are four categories of cards:

### Dance Technique

Each of the 84 orange movement-example cards in the Dance Technique category lists a dance or movement term, a definition of that term, and suggested ways to vary it, called the "Try This" section.

### Sports and Game Movements

Each of the 53 blue movement-example cards displays a sport or game skill, which students are asked to imitate. This category gives nondancers a user-friendly approach to dance. Many sports and game movements have a direct correlation to dance movements; and because both adults and children are more familiar with sports and games than with dance, this category offers a comfortable way to explore choreography. Included are variations to help students move beyond their skill levels and incorporate the skill into dances. Students need not perform the skill to perfection but merely stylize it for use in building a dance. A definition is not included, only some safety tips in the "Try This" section.

### Elements That Change Movements

The 56 green movement-example cards address movement concepts and other factors that can alter a movement or a series of movements. These cards are subcategorized as follows: focus, level, quality, floor pattern, direction, mood, energy, flow of movement, speed, rhythm, and size. Included are a variety of circumstances to help students visualize the listed element.

### Creative Movement Suggestions

The 38 purple movement-example cards can help younger children be creative through guided exploration. The "Try This" section includes situations to inspire students to make their bodies move in different ways. These cards are effective with all age groups, including adults.

## Ways to Use the Cards

A sample card is shown in figure 7.1, with the various parts labeled. The cards can be used in the following ways:

- Select a certain number of cards from each category and combine them to create a movement pattern or dance. The class can work on a dance as a class, in small groups, or individually. You or the students can select specific cards, or you or the students may randomly choose them. Music may or may not be used. (Chapter 3 contains information on how to create dances and should be used in conjunction with this activity.)
- Teach two or three movement skills per lesson, working toward building a bigger dance and movement vocabulary.
- Experiment with the "Try This" section.
- Combine the skills or variations of the skills.
- Organize students in groups of three to five. Give each group a number of cards and have them arrange them in an order. They can lay the cards out on the floor in front of them and try different arrangements. Once the students decide on an order, they should link the movements from each card. Students can use transitions by adding additional movements or by simply moving from one card to the next. They should clearly define the beginning and end of their sequence by freezing the starting

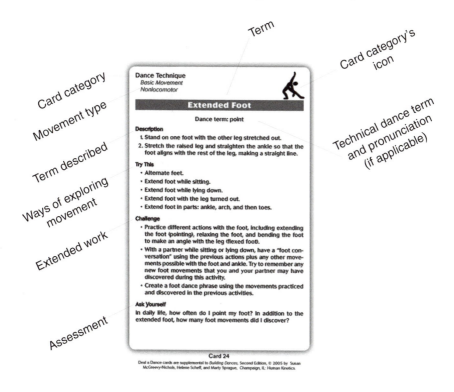

Term

Card category's icon

Card category

Movement type

Term described

Ways of exploring movement

Extended work

Assessment

Technical dance term and pronunciation (if applicable)

**Dance Technique**
*Basic Movement*
*Nonlocomotor*

**Extended Foot**

Dance term: point

**Description**
1. Stand on one foot with the other leg stretched out.
2. Stretch the raised leg and straighten the ankle so that the foot aligns with the rest of the leg, making a straight line.

**Try This**
• Alternate feet.
• Extend foot while sitting.
• Extend foot while lying down.
• Extend foot with the leg turned out.
• Extend foot in parts: ankle, arch, and then toes.

**Challenge**
• Practice different actions with the foot, including extending the foot (pointing), relaxing the foot, and bending the foot to make an angle with the leg (flexed foot).
• With a partner while sitting or lying down, have a "foot conversation" using the previous actions plus any other movements possible with the foot and ankle. Try to remember any new foot movements that you and your partner may have discovered during this activity.
• Create a foot dance phrase using the movements practiced and discovered in the previous activities.

**Ask Yourself**
In daily life, how often do I point my foot? In addition to the extended foot, how many foot movements did I discover?

Card 24

Deal a Dance cards are supplemental to *Building Dances*, Second Edition, © 2005 by Susan McGreevy-Nichols, Helene Scheff, and Marty Sprague, Champaign, IL: Human Kinetics

**FIGURE 7.1**   A sample dance card.

position of the first movement and holding the finish of the last movement. The groups can then perform their dances for one another.

• A specified number of counts (beats) can be assigned to each movement or to the entire sequence of movements.

• To add music to this activity, teach the class to clap out a beat and organize the musical selection for use when choreographing.

• Select a subcategory from the element cards, such as change of focus. Pull all the cards in that subcategory (look up, look down, look right, look left, perform two different focus changes in a row, look around, and look behind). Then plan a lesson around this concept, exploring how changing the focus gives different meaning and emphasis to movement. You can use this method in conjunction with a Dance Technique card or Sports and Game Movements card.

• Have the class do any combination in a canon.

## Sample Activity

This example guides the entire class through the creative process of building a piece of choreography. To start, select four cards for the lesson from only two of the categories (that is, two from Dance Technique and two from Sports and Game Movements:

### Dance Technique

Three-step turn (card 61)

Jazz box (card 63)

Clap (card 72)

### Sports and Game Movements

Kick (card 130)

Read aloud to the students the description from one of the cards. Next, read the description again slowly and ask the students to try the movement as you read it. This activity will improve their listening skills and not put you on the spot to demonstrate (figure 7.2). Repeat this process with the other three cards. Once the students have familiarized themselves with the four movements, they can explore the "Try This" section of the cards. Next, with input from the class, select their favorite or best movement. Decide on an order for the movements and what transition movements, if any, you will need.

**Figure 7.2** Students familiarize themselves with movements from the Deal a Dance cards.

Students then learn and practice the sequence (movement pattern). Once they have mastered the sequence to the best of their capacity, select another card from the Elements That Change Movements category. Encourage students to discuss how the information on this card can vary the dance sequence that's already been established.

Let's say you and the class have built the following combination:

1. Three-step turn to the right, touch the left foot in
2. Jazz box
3. Kick
4. Clap three times

In this combination, each step takes 1 count (beat), for a total of 12 counts. Using an additional 12 counts, students then can do this combination with the other leg leading. This 24-count phrase can be done to music. Adding an Elements That Change Movements (change of focus) card, such as card 137, "look up," the group could decide to look up when doing the touch in, the karate kick, or the last clap. You could then divide the class into two groups, instructing half to observe while the other half performs. You could invite the observers to comment on how the change of focus makes the dance sequence different or more interesting or perhaps gives the choreography an air, attitude, or style. Similarly, you can introduce and use a Creative Movement Suggestions card. For example, if card 215, "reach," is selected, they could do the entire combination with their eyes looking up and hands reaching up as if they were trying to touch the stars. You could also discuss other variations from the "Try This" section.

## Grade Level Suggestions for Creating Deal a Dance

Deal a Dance can be adapted to any age level by varying the presentation and organization of the material. Suggestions for modifications follow.

### Grades K to 4

The range of selection for this age group should be limited. Still, children in this age range enjoy a challenge. (Too many times educators use the excuse that children in these grades are neither experienced enough nor capable of grasping or developing ideas and concepts. Nothing could be further from the truth.) You merely have to organize the material differently and be organized yourself. It is best to teach one skill at a time to the entire group and have the class determine which of the learned skills they will perform and in what order.

## Grades 5 to 8

The children in this age group are very creative, motivated, and capable. They aren't afraid to experiment with any ideas presented to them, and they often have ideas of their own to contribute. They can work with the cards in small groups of three to five and begin to experiment with choreographic forms.

## Grades 9 to 12

These students can be the most reluctant because they yield to peer pressure and are self-conscious despite having great ability. Your challenge is to make students feel comfortable about themselves and the subject matter and to present Deal a Dance in a nonthreatening, nonjudgmental, and fun atmosphere. Students in these grades are capable of working on their own and should experiment with different music, seeing how it affects their choreography.

# Criteria for Assessment

The students' work in the Deal a Dance activity should include the following criteria:

## Movement Skills

✓ Nonlocomotor movements

✓ Locomotor movements

✓ Identify a beat in a variety of music (where applicable)

✓ Use of elements that can change movement

✓ Basic dance movements

✓ Series of movements that form movement patterns and dance phrases

✓ An increased skill level

## Cognitive Skills

✓ Memorization of a sequence of movement

✓ Persistence with task

✓ Constructive comments

✓ Application of decision-making skills

✓ Description of dance using appropriate dance terms

✓ Identification of movement and movement elements occurring in a movement pattern or dance phrase

✓ Identification of choreographic concepts and forms

## Choreographic and Creative Process

✓ Variation of original combination through exploration

✓ Application of music to combination

✓ Use of choreographic forms

✓ Application of choreographic and movement skills to express ideas nonverbally through dance

## Social and Aesthetic Skills

✓ Use of self-direction and self-discipline

✓ Contribution to the group effort

✓ Performance of the finished combination or dance phrase

✓ Observation of others' performances

✓ Sense of accomplishment

When assessing students, base your assessment for this activity on these criteria, or use the sample checklists or assessment forms in chapter 6. The following is a general rubric that you can use to evaluate students' work.

3 = Above standard. Completed all "Try This" suggestions.
   Completed all challenges.
   Completed "Ask Yourself" in written form.

2 = At standard. Completed all "Try This" suggestions.
   Completed one of the challenges.
   Answered "Ask Yourself" in discussion form.

1 = Needs more work. Missing any criteria from the "at standard" level.

# Picture Dance

This activity fulfills the following standards:

National Dance Standards: 1, 2, 3, 4, 5, 7

National Standards for Physical Education: 1, 2, 5, 6

This activity can heighten visual interpretation and observation skills. The process of the activity also builds self-esteem while encouraging teamwork. It allows children with limited English verbal skills to participate with peers.

## Description of Activity or Procedure

The activity uses pictures as a source for the positions and movements used in creating dances. An individual or group imitates the images. Several of these "pictures" are then linked with movement to create movement patterns or small dances. The first step in this activity is to gather pictures from magazines, newspapers, old programs, brochures, and the like. You could have the raw materials on hand or encourage the students to bring them to school. The pictures should be of people in action—dancers, athletes, or anyone who moves.

Next, the students select (or are assigned) a group of pictures. They can work individually or in small groups to establish an order to the pictures. Then the students, alone or with help from you, mimic the images in the pictures and, using the creative process, link the individual images by connecting movements. Music could enhance the whole project, adding another dimension to the creative process.

## Sample Activity

A group of five children selects three pictures—one of a baseball player swinging a bat, another of a horse leaping high over a hurdle, and the last of a person bending over a flower bed. The following is the order that the group decides on:

1. Bending
2. Batting
3. Leaping

In a cooperative effort, all five group members first bend over, then start to rise while twisting their bodies as if to swing a bat, then end the sequence with their version of the horse in midair (figure 7.3). Encourage the group to elaborate on their actions, adding linking movements to make the sequence a beginning piece of choreography.

## Grade Level Suggestions for Creating Picture Dance

Picture Dance can be adapted to any age level by varying the presentation and organization of the material. Suggestions for modifications follow.

### Grades K to 4

While facilitating the class, do the following:

1. Have students work collectively to imitate the images in the pictures. (Their imitations may be very literal.)

2. Encourage them to explore the various ways they can go from one image to another.

### Grades 5 to 8

Students in this age range are capable of working in larger groups and with more pictures.

**Figure 7.3**    In a picture dance activity, students imitate visual images and develop transitions.

1. Give the students a specified number of counts in which to accomplish each position and movement.

2. Give them an appropriate time frame for the linking movements.

3. Encourage them to use the elements of choreography to vary the sequence, such as adding arm movements while bending over, adding a swing as they approach the batting twist, and doing a quick run before the leap.

### Grades 9 to 12

1. Students can take the movements used in grades 5 to 8 and begin to develop a story line around them.

2. They can use additional moves to further develop the story line and make it clearer.

3. They could choose music and make the sequence fit the musical phrasing and make the quality of the movements fit the mood of the music (lyrical, staccato, heavy, light, and so on).

## Criteria for Assessment

The students' work in the Picture Dance activity should include the following criteria:

### Movement Skills

✓ Representation in movement of an image or picture

✓ Organization of movement in logical order

✓ Inclusion of basic movement skills

✓ Combination of series of movements to form movement patterns or dance phrases

### Cognitive Skills

✓ Observation skills

✓ Memorization of a sequence of movements

✓ Persistence with a task

✓ Constructive comments

✓ Application of decision-making skills

## Choreographic and Creative Process

✓ Variation of original combination through exploration of movement

✓ Application of music to movement patterns

## Social and Aesthetic Skills

✓ Use of self-direction and self-discipline

✓ Contribution to the group effort

✓ Performance of the finished combination or dance phrase

✓ Observation of others' performances

✓ Sense of accomplishment

When assessing students, base your assessment for this activity on these criteria, or use the sample checklists or assessment forms in chapter 6. A general rubric that can be used for evaluating students' work follows.

3 = Above standard. Completed all "Try This" suggestions.

Completed all challenges.

Completed "Ask Yourself" in written form.

2 = At standard. Completed all "Try This" suggestions.

Completed one of the challenges.

Answered "Ask Yourself" in discussion form.

1 = Needs more work. Missing any criteria from the "at standard" level.

# Words, Sentences, and Paragraphs

This activity fulfills the following standards:

National Dance Standards: 1, 2, 3, 4, 7

National Standards for Physical Education: 1, 2, 5, 6

This activity lends itself to team teaching with a literacy, English, or bilingual teacher. The activity is a wonderful bridge between native languages and English in schools where children are bilingual or have limited English-language skills; in situations where students have poor language skills, it can help raise the literacy level by introducing concepts through a fun, nonthreatening activity. For young students with preverbal skills, the activity also furnishes a means of expression.

## Description of Activity or Procedure

A dance or sport movement is assigned a specific word, either in English or the student's native language. These individual words are then linked together to form a sentence, and sentences are linked to form a paragraph.

## Sample Activity

Let's say *The sky is blue!* is the lead sentence in what is to become a paragraph. Figure 7.4 shows children performing the movements for this opening sentence. The move represented by the word *sky* is a standing layout. The word *is* is a standing straddle with hands on hips, and the move represented by *blue* is a tuck, or squat. The students can then perform the movements according to the order of the words.

The next sentence is *The blue sky turns dark when it is going to rain.* Again, *blue* is a tuck (the student can stay in the position from the previous sentence or rise and tuck again); *sky* is a standing layout; *turns* is a jump half turn; *dark* is a stride position with hands over face; *going* is a run; and *rain* is a leap.

The closing sentence is *The rain from the dark sky makes the flowers grow.* Once again, *rain* is a leap; *from* is a pulling in of arms to chest; *dark* is the stride position with hands over face; *sky* is a standing layout; *makes* is a clap; *flowers* is a kneel on one knee with arms

**Figure 7.4** Students perform movements for the sentence *The sky is blue.*

stretched overhead; and *grow* is a slow rise. This sentence marks the end of the paragraph.

You read the paragraph, and the students perform the appropriate movements for each word. This activity provides a progression of both thought and movement. The sentence is factual, so learning is taking place. As words from one sentence are carried into the other, a feeling of continuity and movement results.

## Grade Level Suggestions for Creating Words, Sentences, and Paragraphs Dance

Words, Sentences, and Paragraphs can be adapted to any age level by varying the presentation and organization of the material. Suggestions for modifications follow.

### Grades K to 4

1. Groups of students portray different words through movement.

2. These students develop simple movement sentences or movement phrases.

3. Second- and third-graders can perform their sentences in a sequence to form a short movement paragraph or dance section.

## Grades 5 to 8

1. Do step 1 from grades K to 4.

2. Arrange the students in rows and then group the sets of rows. (Each group represents a specific word in the paragraph.)

3. As you read the paragraph, the members of each group execute their word, holding a position after they move. Students must not move when it is not their word.

4. The action should move from stage right to stage left and from upstage to downstage as when one reads text on a page. An example follows:

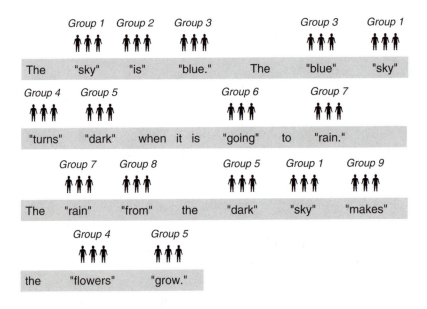

| Group 1 | Group 2 | Group 3 | | Group 3 | Group 1 |
|---------|---------|---------|----|---------|---------|
| The | "sky" | "is" | "blue."  The | "blue" | "sky" |

| Group 4 | Group 5 | | Group 6 | Group 7 |
|---------|---------|------------|---------|---------|
| "turns" | "dark" | when it is | "going" to | "rain." |

| | Group 7 | Group 8 | | Group 5 | Group 1 | Group 9 |
|--|---------|---------|-----|---------|---------|---------|
| The | "rain" | "from" | the | "dark" | "sky" | "makes" |

| | Group 4 | Group 5 |
|--|---------|---------|
| the | "flowers" | "grow." |

5. Use additional movements as punctuation marks. Individual students or all students can perform them—it's your choice.

## Grades 9 to 12

1. Ask groups of students to choose a paragraph from a famous piece of literature.

2. Each group should follow steps 1 to 5 from grades 5 to 8.

3. Students should recite the words while they are dancing to create a spoken text.

4. Have the students share their work with classmates.

# Criteria for Assessment

The students' work in the Word, Sentences, and Paragraph activity should include the following criteria:

## Movement Skills

✓ Representation of words in movement

✓ Addition to personal movement vocabulary

✓ Series of movements to form movement patterns and dance phrases

✓ Inclusion of movement elements and skills

## Cognitive Skills

✓ Memorization of a sequence of movement patterns

✓ Persistence with task

✓ Constructive comments

✓ Use of simple sentence structure

✓ Use of paragraph structure

## Choreographic and Creative Process

✓ Movements that represent words, thoughts, and ideas

✓ Variation of original combination while exploring movement

## Social and Aesthetic Skills

✓ Use of self-direction and self-discipline

✓ Contribution to the group effort

✓ Performance of the finished combination or dance phrase

✓ Observation of others' performances

✓ Sense of accomplishment

When assessing students, base your assessment for this activity on these criteria, or use the sample checklists or assessment forms in chapter 6. A general rubric that can be used for evaluating students' work follows.

3 = Above standard. Completed all "Try This" suggestions.

Completed all challenges.

Completed "Ask Yourself" in written form.

2 = At standard. Completed all "Try This" suggestions.

Completed one of the challenges.

Answered "Ask Yourself" in discussion form.

1 = Needs more work. Missing any criteria from the "at standard" level.

## Story Dance

This activity fulfills the following standards:
National Dance Standards: 1, 2, 3, 4, 7
National Standards for Physical Education: 1, 2, 5, 6

This activity contributes to the development of nonverbal communication and the ability to develop story lines. It can also create opportunities for team teaching and be a means of collaborative teaching with you taking part in the planning. Children of any age can create their own story from simple facts you give them. You could also choose a theme, such as "Taking a Trip" or "Saving Our Oceans." We've included suggestions for ways to build a story based on a theme. For example, meet with the English teacher and learn what literature the children are reading while you are doing this unit. From *Mr. Popper's Penguins* in the elementary grades to *Little House on the Prairie* in the middle grades to *Romeo and Juliet* and *Old Man and the Sea* in the upper grades, the challenge of bringing these pieces of literature to life nonverbally is exciting. This project is also an ongoing one that enhances memory as well as interpretive skills.

One way of enticing children to think about the project from one class period to the next is to make the story grow each time. The children can add new dimensions and twists to the stories they create. The possibilities are endless.

## Description of Activity or Procedure

Portray a story, either existing or original, through movement. For this activity, someone supplies a story that is age appropriate and of interest to the students, who then read the story or who have it read to them. Through a series of movements, mime, and a display of feelings, they should depict the story nonverbally, working independently or as teams. They are to create movement patterns and combinations of steps that help them to relate the story to their "listeners."

Students are eager and capable of doing their own research on a given theme. An effective method of drawing information and ideas from children is brainstorming, an exciting process for both students and teacher. Give the students subcategories within a theme. If your theme is "Saving Our Oceans," the subcategories might be jobs, fun things to do, and sea life. Then the children, as quickly as they can, shout out words and phrases in a specific subcategory. Record the suggestions on a blackboard or an easel pad so that all the students can see and more easily remember what has already been suggested. Limit brainstorming sessions to five-minute periods, and explain that although the shouting-out part of this exercise is acceptable in this situation, it is not always acceptable during regular class activities. Your students can then explore these ideas in various ways through movement.

## Sample Activity: Goldilocks and the Three Bears

Team effort: Three people are chosen or volunteer to be the bears, and one person can be Goldilocks. To be fair, you may want to pick names out of a hat. You or the team decides which version of the story is to be told. Figure 7.5 shows students depicting a critical moment in the plot through movement.

The children decide which movement skills would best depict Papa Bear, Mama Bear, and Baby Bear. Maybe the baby would skip; Mama would take light and delicate steps; and Papa would take big,

**Figure 7.5** Students perform *Goldilocks and the Three Bears* as a story dance.

heavy, plodding steps. They could then go through the motions of going out into the forest for a picnic or a walk while the porridge cools. They could incorporate movements done in a circle or use a blanket as a prop, raising and lowering it as part of the preparation for the picnic.

Meanwhile, Goldilocks would enter the scene. She could be frightened (cautious lunging steps) or exhilarated by the fresh air and take skipping, jumping, and leaping steps until she discovers the home of the three bears. Her focus would then be that of investigation and discovery—tasting, trying the chairs, and finally going to bed and sleeping. She could use stretches, extended movements, and slow motion to depict fatigue.

The bears re-enter and discover the half-eaten cereal, the broken chair, and finally the intruder in the bed. The children could decide all the movement patterns or, depending on the situation, you could give direct input. Though this example is simplistic, considerable leeway exists for more creativity in the story dance activity.

All of these verbal exercises now translate into movement patterns and eventually into a story ballet. (A story ballet doesn't mean that the dance discipline need be ballet. All dances that tell a story are called ballets.)

## Grade Level Suggestion for Creating Story Dance

Story Dance can be adapted to any age level by varying the presentation and organization of the material. Suggestions for modifications follow.

### Grades K to 4
1. The students can decide on a story theme. The research is done for them, or it can be a team effort between teacher and students.

2. Students can take the events, begin to put them in a logical order, and (with help from you) develop movements and movement phrases based on these events.

3. The students can make up several ending movement phrases.

4. Students vote on which ending they like best.

### Grades 5 to 8
1. Discuss the "serial" and "cliff-hanger" methods of story telling (for example, the soap opera).

2. The story dance should be developed in such a way that it can be performed in segments using a narrator, pleading with the audience to stay tuned for the next exciting episode.

## Grades 9 to 12

1. Students in these grades can come up with their own theme or story line.

2. Students can build the story dance in conjunction with any other subject area, giving the whole unit a broader scope.

3. Once the story dance is complete, students can perform it for other classes, for other schools, and for the community.

# Criteria for Assessment

The students' work in the Story Dance activity should include the following criteria:

## Movement Skills

✓ Represent a story line through movement

✓ Addition to personal movement vocabulary

✓ Series of movements to form movement patterns and dance phrases

✓ Use of the body as an instrument for expression and communication

## Cognitive Skills

✓ Memorization of a sequence of movement patterns

✓ Persistence with a task

✓ Constructive comments

✓ Evidence of brainstorming strategies

✓ Evidence of research skills

✓ Inclusion of research, written work, and performance

## Choreographic and Creative Process

✓ Movements that represent words, thoughts, and ideas; variation of original combination while exploring movement

✓ Own ideas shown in dance making and performance

✓ Application of choreographic concepts to express ideas nonverbally through dance

✓ Creation and development of a story line

## Social and Aesthetic Skills

✓ Use of self-direction and self-discipline

✓ Contribution to the group effort

✓ Performance of the finished combination or dance phrase

✓ Observation of others' performances

✓ Sense of accomplishment

When assessing students, base your assessment for this activity on these criteria, or use the sample checklists or assessment forms in chapter 6. A general rubric that can be used for evaluating students' work follows.

3 = Above standard. Completed all "Try This" suggestions.

Completed all challenges.

Completed "Ask Yourself" in written form.

2 = At standard. Completed all "Try This" suggestions.

Completed one of the challenges.

Answered "Ask Yourself" in discussion form.

1 = Needs more work. Missing any criteria from the "at standard" level.

# Write What I See

This activity fulfills the following standards:
National Dance Standards: 1, 2, 3, 4, 7
National Standards for Physical Education: 1, 2, 5, 6

This activity hones observation and listening skills while enhancing literacy skills.

## Description of Activity or Procedure

A student assumes a position while others accurately describe that position in writing. A student who did not see it then re-creates the position based on the written description.

Establish two teams and place them in opposite areas of the room. One person from each team assumes a pose, and the other students on that team describe the pose in writing exactly as they see it. This written description can be in a list or paragraph form. The teams swap writing descriptions. One student on the team reads the description while another student on the team tries to re-create the pose.

## Sample Activity

Child A stands in an arabesque (scale) position (card 92) on the right foot with the left leg stretched out behind, the knee straight, and the foot extended. The arms are in front of the body, with elbows bent at a 90-degree angle and palms facing up. The head is lifted to the ceiling. Child B writes that child A is standing on one foot with the other leg behind. The arms are bent (figure 7.6).

While this is taking place, child C and child D are doing the same thing. Team 1 (A and B) and team 2 (C and D) then swap written descriptions. Child C reads team 1's description to child D, who tries to re-enact the original position of child A based on what is being read. All students sit and watch, and you then ask the child who was the original demonstrator whether the position shown is correct. If it is not accurate, then the original demonstrator should show exactly how it should look. You then discuss with the class how the written description must be altered and elaborated to match the original pose.

**Figure 7.6**   In a Write What I See activity, students write descriptions of poses.

## Grade Level Suggestions for Creating Write What I See Dance

Write What I See can be adapted to any age level by varying the presentation and organization of the material. Suggestions for modifications follow.

### Grades K to 4

1. Students could tell what they observed while you record what they say on a blackboard or easel pad.

2. Have a trio of students leave the room or go to the other side of the room with their backs turned while this activity is going on. The children are then invited back, and the description is read while the children re-create it.

3. The group makes corrections as a whole, and you discuss vocabulary and the importance of being specific about what they see.

### Grades 5 to 8

1. Students would follow the sample activity, substituting their own shapes.
2. Place greater emphasis on written skills such as clarity and order of the steps through the movement procedure.
3. Have students link poses to make a movement phrase.

### Grades 9 to 12

1. Students can split into groups of three consisting of a recorder, a describer, and a demonstrator.
2. Each group does the sample activity, substituting their own shapes and simple movements.
3. Place greater emphasis on vocabulary, grammar, and sentence structure.
4. Have the groups link all poses to create a class dance.

## Criteria for Assessment

The students' work of the Write What I See activity should include the following criteria:

### Movement Skills

✓ Addition to personal movement vocabulary

✓ Use of elements that change movements

✓ Use of movement elements and skills

### Cognitive Skills

✓ Observation skills

✓ Memorization of a sequence of movements

✓ Persistence with a task

✓ Constructive comments

✓ Application of decision-making skills

✓ Evidence of listening skills

✓ Evidence of writing skills

### Choreographic and Creative Process

✓ Use of a series of positions to create a movement pattern

## Social and Aesthetic Skills

✓ Use of self-direction and self-discipline

✓ Contribution to the group effort

✓ Performance of the finished combination or dance phrase

✓ Observation of others' performances

✓ Sense of accomplishment

When assessing students, base your assessment for this activity on these criteria, or use the sample checklists or assessment forms in chapter 6. A general rubric that can be used for evaluating students' work follows.

3 = Above standard. Completed all "Try This" suggestions.

Completed all challenges.

Completed "Ask Yourself" in written form.

2 = At standard. Completed all "Try This" suggestions.

Completed one of the challenges.

Answered "Ask Yourself" in discussion form.

1 = Needs more work. Missing any criteria from the "at standard" level.

# Machine Dance

This activity fulfills the following standards:
National Dance Standards: 1, 2, 3, 4, 7
National Standards for Physical Education: 1, 2, 5, 6

This activity helps develop students' conceptualization skills while increasing spatial and kinesthetic awareness. It also enhances the creative process through problem solving, teamwork, and cooperative thinking.

## Description of Activity or Procedure

Groups of students act out the movements of a machine using the concept of gears and action and reaction. For this activity the students need to come up with a machine, either real or imagined. Divide the class into working groups of three to five students. Odd numbers seem to work the best. The groups can all decide on one machine, or each group can develop one on its own.

Using their bodies, students create the parts of the machine. They then need to show how one "gear" is dependent on another to work. One child starts by moving the part that links to the next child, and then the next, and so on. When each group has completed the task, you can then link all the groups around the perimeter of the room, making one gigantic automaton.

## Sample Activity

Student A stands with both hands on hips, facing forward. His right arm swings across his chest, turning him one half revolution to the left, where he taps the shoulder of student B, who was standing with his back toward the front of the room. Student B bends in half from the waist, sending his right arm to the side, where it touches the head of student C, who is sitting on the floor, curled up, with his back to student B. Student C, when tapped on the head, unfolds, stretching his arms and legs out to either side, where they make contact with students D and E, who then do a forward roll at the same time but in different directions (figure 7.7).

**FIGURE 7.7** In a Machine Dance, students interact like moving parts of a machine.

To take this one step further, as you add students you can eventually return to the first person, who starts the sequence over from the beginning. You can also add a "problem" to the task by asking the students to handle a prop while passing it through the machine.

To take it even further, you can add music. The students then have the added job of making their moves fit the rhythm of the music. By changing the music, the students will find that their "machine" may act very differently.

## Grade Level Suggestions for Creating Machine Dance

Machine Dance can be adapted to any age level by varying the presentation and organization of the material. Suggestions for modifications follow.

### Grades K to 4

1. Students can create several "gear" moves and share them with the class.

2. The class would then explain how they would connect these moves.

3. Each student could choose one of the gears he or she wanted to be, and the machine would work in a circle so that they could see each other.

4. They could take a field trip to watch an automatic car wash or bottling plant so that they could watch actual gears in action.

### Grades 5 to 8

1. Brainstorm different movements that machine parts do (up and down, around, side to side, in and out).

2. Using the movement from the brainstorming session, students create a complicated imaginary machine or assembly line. (A good resource is the movie *Charlie and the Chocolate Factory*. They could also make a field trip to an automobile assembly line or a factory that uses robotics to assemble a product.)

### Grades 9 to 12

1. Students could build a dance based on a project from their physics or science class, or they could observe an actual machine in motion. (They could visit a vocational education class to observe a machine.)

2. They could then analyze the different parts, seeing what makes them work and how they work. Their bodies would simulate those parts, acting and interacting with other parts to re-create the working machine they saw.

## Criteria for Assessment

The students' work of the Machine Dance activity should include the following criteria:

### Movement Skills

✓ Representation in movement of an image or picture

✓ Organization of movement in logical order

✓ Inclusion of movement elements and skills

✓ Combination of series of movements to form movement patterns and dance phrases

### Cognitive Skills

✓ Observation skills

✓ Memorization of a sequence of movements

✓ Persistence with a task

✓ Constructive comments

✓ Application of decision-making skills

## Choreographic and Creative Process

✓ Variation of original combination through exploration of movement

✓ Application of music to movement patterns

## Social and Aesthetic Skills

✓ Use of self-direction and self-discipline

✓ Contribution to the group effort

✓ Performance of the finished combination or dance phrase

✓ Observation of others' performances

✓ Sense of accomplishment

When assessing students, base your assessment for this activity on these criteria, or use the sample checklists or assessment forms in chapter 6. A general rubric that can be used for evaluating students' work follows.

3 = Above standard. Completed all "Try This" suggestions.
   Completed all challenges.
   Completed "Ask Yourself" in written form.

2 = At standard. Completed all "Try This" suggestions.
   Completed one of the challenges.
   Answered "Ask Yourself" in discussion form.

1 = Needs more work. Missing any criteria from the "at standard" level.

# Costume and Prop Dance

This activity fulfills the following standards:
National Dance Standards: 1, 2, 3, 4, 5, 7
National Standards for Physical Education: 1, 2, 5, 6

This activity helps students realize that people can be different from their images. Students can use open-ended statements such as "A motorcycle jacket means the person in it acts . . ." or "A velvet hat with a feather means the person wearing it is . . ." The typical finish to the first statement could be "tough and crude." A finish for the second statement could be "haughty and snobbish." But in reality, we know people who wear motorcycle clothes may be gentle and caring, and women with feathers in their hats may just be making a fashion statement. While the activity develops creative-thinking and observation skills, it also gives the students confidence in making decisions and makes them aware of their capabilities. On a social note, we as a society tend to prejudge people based on their actions and clothes. We might predetermine that someone in overalls won't like opera or someone who drives a hot rod cannot possibly be a bank executive. This activity helps students at all levels debate these preconceptions. Costume and Prop Dance uses a form of improvisation and helps children with development of a character. They act out what they feel about people who look a certain way and how they think people perceive the character they are portraying.

## Description of Activity or Procedure

Students select costume pieces or props that inspire them to create a character through movement. For this activity you need to have a bag of tricks—a collection of hats, scarves, jackets, jewelry, accessories, books, writing implements, purses, and pocket items. The first time around, have the children choose one or two articles from the bag and ask them to create a character from these costume pieces or props. They can write down the characteristics or just keep them in their heads. Have them tell you about the person they are creating, then they move as they believe their character would.

The next step is to have these characters interact. They can develop a situation and resolve it through dance and movement.

## Sample Activity

Johnny chooses a baseball cap and a stopwatch. He puts the cap on backward with the beak down against his neck. He puts the stopwatch cord around his wrist and the watch in the palm of his hand. He thus becomes a game manager—tough at every angle and precise to the extreme. He develops moves that are forceful, angular, and exacting (figure 7.8).

Tina chooses a sequined tiara and feather boa. She wraps the boa around her neck and tilts her head into the air. She takes on the air of a showgirl—sophisticated, arrogant, self-controlled, but she's mildly self-conscious. She parades around the room, strutting her stuff, but she's really worried about what the public will think of her. Johnny and Tina could then develop a problem that would cause them to interact. Maybe they could switch props and empathize with the other's problems.

## Grade Level Suggestions for Creating Costume and Prop Dance

Costume and Prop Dance can be adapted to any age level by varying the presentation and organization of the material. Suggestions for modifications follow.

**Figure 7.8** Props help convey character.

## Grades K to 4

1. Have the children get into a circle.

2. Place a costume piece or prop in the center.

3. Ask students to react to it with movement, either one at a time or all at the same time. (Standing in a circle helps keep them focused. Ask students to freeze while you change the object in the middle of the circle.)

4. Students should memorize each movement reaction and then combine these movements to form a small dance.

## Grades 5 to 8

The more outlandish the prop, the more creative the students seem to be. After the students become comfortable with the activity, you can do the choosing for them. Selecting props that are not necessarily within their frame of reference broadens their thinking and encourages them to explore new feelings and images for the characters behind the props.

## Grades 9 to 12

1. Have the students think of and demonstrate traits and characteristics of a person they have in mind, using some of the skills they developed through Deal a Dance. Let them tell you what props they need in order to make the characterization clearer.

2. You could also add the element of music. Each character freezes "on stage" while one does the dance. You can change the music for each character or have them react to the same music but in the way they believe their character would. After each of the characters is introduced, they could also interact.

# Criteria for Assessment

The students' work of the Costume and Prop Dance activity should include the following criteria:

## Movement Skills

✓ Use of the body as an instrument for expression and communication through movement

✓ Use of movement elements and skills

✓ Combination of a series of movements to form movement patterns and dance phrases

✓ Addition to personal movement vocabulary

## Cognitive Skills

✓ Observation skills

✓ Memorization of a sequence of movements

✓ Persistence with a task

✓ Constructive comments

✓ Application of decision-making skills

## Choreographic and Creative Process

✓ Variation of original combination while exploring movement

✓ Application of music to movement patterns

✓ Application of choreographic and movement skills to express ideas nonverbally in dance

## Social and Aesthetic Skills

✓ Use of self-direction and self-discipline

✓ Contribution to the group effort

✓ Performance of the finished combination or dance phrase

✓ Observation of others' performances

✓ Sense of accomplishment

When assessing students, base your assessment for this activity on these criteria, or use the sample checklists or assessment forms in chapter 6. A general rubric that can be used for evaluating students' work follows.

3 = Above standard. Completed all "Try This" suggestions.

Completed all challenges.

Completed "Ask Yourself" in written form.

2 = At standard. Completed all "Try This" suggestions.

Completed one of the challenges.

Answered "Ask Yourself" in discussion form.

1 = Needs more work. Missing any criteria from the "at standard" level.

# Decode a Dance

This activity fulfills the following standards:
  National Dance Standards: 1, 2, 3, 4, 5, 7
  National Standards for Physical Education: 1, 2, 5, 6

Decode a Dance develops interpretation skills from body language to the spoken or written word and from mind to body to paper. It increases students' appreciation of music, and they learn how different kinds of music enhance expression. Having older students help the younger ones fosters a cooperative learning experience and develops role models.

## Description of Activity or Procedure

Some students perform an untitled dance. Other students who are observing write a narrative of their interpretation the dance. This decoding can yield different meanings from different people.

For this activity, one student will need to have a vision of a dance or a concept of the desired result. This person, the choreographer, creates a sentence, paragraph, or entire story using dance and movement vocabulary. Several students can take part. The other students become the observers, decoding the story as it evolves. They can describe actions, feelings, relationships, and any other thoughts. As the scene is developed and refined, the choreographer could choose appropriate music, and the observers could comment on how the music helped or hindered the dance concept.

## Sample Activity

Three students are "on stage," and one is sitting curled up, as in figure 7.9. The second student begins to shiver and shake, moving the arms as if to get warmer. The third student "blows in" on the scene with a flurry and lands on the curled-up student. The students observing develop the following scenario: A snowball sits on the ground. The flapping student symbolizes the cold. The third student is more snow landing on the snowball, making it larger.

**FIGURE 7.9**   Choreography for a snow scene.

## Grade Level Suggestions
## for Creating Decode a Dance

Decode a Dance can be adapted to any age level by varying the presentation and organization of the material. Suggestions for modifications follow.

### Grades K to 4

You could have an older class of observers tell the performing class of K to 4 what they believe the scene depicts. The observers could also be asked to write it out and compare all the versions that were "seen." They then explain and describe the scene to the younger class. The older students could also discuss and demonstrate how dance movements would tell the story. Conversely, the K to 4 class could observe an older class and, using verbal skills, tell what the scene meant to them.

### Grades 5 to 8

Half of the class could write out the version of the scene being performed by the other half, thereby "decoding" what they see.

### Grades 9 to 12

An English class can be the forum used for introducing critiquing skills. Critique forms can be found in chapter 6.

# Criteria for Assessment

The students' work of the Decode a Dance activity should include the following criteria:

### Movement Skills

✓ Use of the body as an instrument for expression and communication through movement

✓ Use of movement elements and skills

✓ Combination of a series of movements to form movement patterns and dance phrases

✓ Addition to personal movement vocabulary

### Cognitive Skills

✓ Observation skills

✓ Memorization of a sequence of movements

✓ Persistence with a task

✓ Constructive comments

✓ Application of decision-making skills

### Choreographic and Creative Process

✓ Variation of original combination while exploring movement

✓ Application of music to movement patterns

✓ Application of choreographic and movement skills to express ideas nonverbally in dance

### Social and Aesthetic Skills

✓ Use of self-direction and self-discipline

✓ Contribution to the group effort

✓ Performance of the finished combination or dance phrase

✓ Observation of others' performances

✓ Sense of accomplishment

When assessing students, base your assessment for this activity on these criteria, or use the sample checklists or assessment forms in chapter 6. A general rubric that can be used for evaluating students' work follows.

3 = Above standard. Completed all "Try This" suggestions.

Completed all challenges.

Completed "Ask Yourself" in written form.

2 = At standard. Completed all "Try This" suggestions.

Completed one of the challenges.

Answered "Ask Yourself" in discussion form.

1 = Needs more work. Missing any criteria from the "at standard" level.

# Create a Culture

This activity fulfills the following standards:
    National Dance Standards: 1, 2, 3, 4, 5, 6, 7
    National Standards for Physical Education: 1, 2, 3, 5, 6

Create a Culture teaches interviewing, research, and interpersonal communication skills. Students learn what culture is and develop an understanding of cultural diversity and how it positively influences our lives. They also learn cultural or folk dance skills. This activity is a perfect vehicle for team teaching; students and teachers in social studies, bilingual, and English classes would be able to make great contributions.

## Description of Activity or Procedure

The class as a whole creates a fictitious culture and then creates a dance that this culture might do.

Ask students to define culture and describe the components that make up a culture, such as religion, environment, diet, and customs. They then research various cultures and cultural dance forms, their structures, and what the movements represent. Also ask them to interview family or community members who might know of dances and dance movements within their own cultures. Students then share the information, giving the class an understanding of what culture is. Finally, the class creates a fictitious culture, either individually, in groups, or as a class project.

Identify the purpose of the dance in the fictitious culture. For example, is it a harvest, rain, celebration, or perhaps rite-of-passage dance? Then make up movements that represent the type of dance to be created. Once a structure is decided, have the class order movements within the structure and perform the dance.

## Sample Activity

The created culture is from an island with a hot and dry climate. The people are small in stature and strict vegetarians. The soil is poor and not conducive to agriculture, and a staple of their diet is a large fruit that is picked from a tree. To eat this fruit, the people have to break it open by pounding it on the rocks.

**FIGURE 7.10**   A Create a Culture harvest dance.

The dance created is a harvest dance. The people are placed in a circle, and the movements that depict the harvest are reaching to pick, pounding on the rocks, thanking the gods, and eating (figure 7.10).

# Grade Level Suggestions for Creating Create a Culture Dance

Create a Culture can be adapted to any age level by varying the presentation and organization of the material. Suggestions for modifications follow.

### Grades K to 4

Have the students talk about their individual cultures, including when and why they dance in that culture. You could also introduce a folk tale and create a dance to go with some event in the story.

### Grades 5 to 8

You might choose what event this dance represents, such as a celebration or harvest. Then create movements that represent activities done during that event, such as worshiping, gathering food, or the birth of a child. You could also create the aspects of the culture that influence the event, such as climate, religion, customs, and food.

### Grades 9 to 12

Create a culture to be part of an international festival of diversity. Students design costumes, bring recipes that they have developed for this culture, invent a language, and create artifacts and music for the culture. They then perform a dance or series of dances based on this created culture.

## Criteria for Assessment

The students' work of the Create a Culture activity should include the following criteria:

### Movement Skills

✓ Use of the body as an instrument for expression and communication through movement

✓ Use of movement elements and skills

✓ A series of movements to form movement patterns

✓ Addition to personal movement vocabulary

✓ Representation of a story line through movement

✓ Variation of the quality of movement through change of expression

✓ Memorization of a dance learned outside of class

### Cognitive Skills

✓ Observation skills

✓ Memorization of a sequence of movements

✓ Persistence with a task

✓ Constructive comments

✓ Application of decision-making skills

✓ Translation of movement into words

✓ Use of interviewing techniques

✓ Evidence of research included in written work and performance

✓ Evidence of understanding of a culture and how it is influenced by climate, religion, customs, and diet

### Choreographic and Creative Process

✓ Variation of original combination while exploring movement

✓ Interpretation of choreographic concepts used to express ideas nonverbally through dance

✓ Representation through movements to portray words, thoughts, and ideas

✓ Creation of a fictitious culture

✓ Evidence of own ideas in dance making

## Social and Aesthetic Skills

✓ Self-direction and self-discipline

✓ Contribution to the group effort

✓ Performance of the finished combination or dance phrase

✓ Observation of others' performances

✓ Constructive comments

✓ Sense of accomplishment

✓ Evidence of an increased cultural awareness

✓ Appreciation of others' abilities and feelings

When assessing students, base your assessment for this activity on these criteria, or use the sample checklists or assessment forms in chapter 6. A general rubric that can be used for evaluating students' work follows.

3 = Above standard. Completed all "Try This" suggestions.

Completed all challenges.

Completed "Ask Yourself" in written form.

2 = At standard. Completed all "Try This" suggestions.

Completed one of the challenges.

Answered "Ask Yourself" in discussion form.

1 = Needs more work. Missing any criteria from the "at standard" level.

# On the Move Dance

This activity fulfills the following standards:
    National Dance Standards: 1, 2, 3, 4, 5, 7
    National Standards for Physical Education: 1, 2, 5, 6

Through this activity children learn about speed, direction changes, and force while also delving into many modes of transportation from the beginning of time to the present. You will end up with a "moving" dance.

## Description of Activity or Procedure

Look at various modes of transportation from the beginning of time to modern-day space travel. Working in teams, students bring these modes of transportation to life through movement.

## Sample Activity

Read or write a story about transportation. (For K to 4, you could use *The Little Engine That Could*). Explore with the class how the body would depict the movement of the selected modes of transportation. Arrange and order the movement phrases to reflect the story line.

Examples of modes of transportation are beasts of burden (such as plow horses and donkeys), wagons, steamboats and steam engines, water vehicles, underwater vehicles, air and outer-space vehicles, mass-transit vehicles, and all-terrain vehicles.

## Grade Level Suggestions for Creating On the Move Dance

On the Move Dance can be adapted to any age level by varying the presentation and organization of the material. Suggestions for modifications follow.

### Grades K to 4

1. Discuss a few simple vehicles.
2. From those discussed, select two different means of transportation (such as a steam locomotive and a tricycle).

3. Explore the characteristics of each of the two (puffing, bound by track; balancing, leg driven).

4. Have half the class work as steam locomotives and the rest as tricycles. As individuals they create simple movements for their vehicles.

5. With you facilitating, arrange the movements contributed by the students.

6. Have the two teams interact as the vehicles they are depicting.

## Grades 5 to 8

1. Look at layouts of different airport terminals. They are usually designed to accommodate many airline companies. Some airports are designed in spokelike configurations, while others have different shapes. These shapes can be used to create formations and patterns.

2. Tour a local airport and ask about different kinds of planes (or take a virtual tour of an airport and planes on the Internet)

3. Write about situations that might occur when you have a certain number of runways and a certain number of planes taking off and landing. You can add weather as a factor.

4. Have students devise movement phrases depicting different planes and create a map for the takeoffs and landings.

5. Create a dance using the movement patterns and maps from step 4.

6. Add music to the mix.

## Grades 9 to 12

1. Research outer-space vehicles.

2. Students divide into groups of 5.

3. Students create a scenario (story or scene) and write a script.

4. Students create movement signatures and phrases for the people and things in the scenario (such as spaceships, extraterrestrial vehicles, clouds, storms).

5. Students link movement phrases to verbal phrases, creating a dance.

6. Add music and perform.

## Criteria for Assessment

The students' work of On the Move activity should include the following criteria:

### Movement Skills

✓ Use of the body as an instrument for expression and communication through movement

✓ Use of movement elements and skills

✓ A series of movements to form movement patterns

✓ Addition to personal movement vocabulary

✓ Representation of a story line through movement

✓ Variation of the quality of movement through change of expression

### Cognitive Skills

✓ Observation skills

✓ Memorization of a sequence of movements

✓ Persistence with a task

✓ Constructive comments

✓ Application of decision-making skills

✓ Translation of movement into words

✓ Use of interviewing techniques

✓ Evidence of research included in written work and performance

### Choreographic and Creative Process

✓ Variation of original combination while exploring movement

✓ Interpretation of choreographic concepts used to express ideas nonverbally through dance

✓ Representation through movements to portray words, thoughts, and ideas

✓ Evidence of own ideas in dance making

### Social and Aesthetic Skills

✓ Self-direction and self-discipline

✓ Contribution to the group effort

✓ Performance of the finished combination or dance phrase

✓ Observation of others' performance

✓ Constructive comments

✓ Sense of accomplishment

When assessing students, base your assessment for this activity on these criteria, or use the sample checklists or assessment forms in chapter 6. A general rubric that can be used for evaluating students' work follows.

3 = Above standard. Completed all "Try This" suggestions.

Completed all challenges.

Completed "Ask Yourself" in written form.

2 = At standard. Completed all "Try This" suggestions.

Completed one of the challenges.

Answered "Ask Yourself" in discussion form.

1 = Needs more work. Missing any criteria from the "at standard" level.

# Holiday Dance

This activity fulfills the following standards:
National Dance Standards: 1, 2, 3, 4, 5, 7
National Standards for Physical Education: 1, 2, 5, 6

Dance has traditionally been a part of holiday celebrations. Through this activity students can develop or share dances that celebrate holidays.

## Description of Activity or Procedure

Celebrate holidays around the world through movement. For this activity, students need to research and report on holidays from different cultures. Students create symbolic movements to depict a holiday, and they know why people dance to celebrate the occasion.

## Sample Activity

May Day was originally a Russian holiday. Students research why it was celebrated. A leading question could be why people in the United States stopped celebrating it for a period of time. The maypole dance was a tradition for centuries; students can find information in traditional research sources and on the Internet. They then create an actual maypole and create dances that intertwine the ribbons. Of course, if this were a full-blown festival in the school, they could create festive costumes.

## Grade Level Suggestions for Creating Holiday Dance

Holiday Dance can be adapted to any age level by varying the presentation and organization of the material. Suggestions for modifications follow.

### Grades K to 4

1. Have students discuss their favorite holidays.
2. Select one of these holidays and have students read stories about it to see how it is celebrated.
3. Have students brainstorm why a dance could be part of the holiday celebration. (For example, if you choose Veterans Day

you could create a victory march and use the music of John Philip Sousa.)

4. When the students complete the brainstorm activity and decide, with your input, what form the dance would take, they create movements and movement patterns.

5. Work as a group to arrange these movements and patterns in order to create a dance.

### Grades 5 to 8

1. In small groups, students research a holiday that is not part of their tradition.

2. Once the groups decide on a specific holiday, they write, using their research, about the special features of the celebration. They could also research appropriate music that may be recorded. Suppose they chose the Swedish holiday of St. Lucia's Day. They learned that the little girls and teenage girls wear boughs of leaves in their hair and that candles are woven into these leaves. How would they have to hold their heads so that the candles would not fall?

3. Students could decide what form the dance takes and create movements and movement patterns. The boys in the group have to research what part in the celebration they would play. Perhaps it is the serving of those wonderful St. Lucia's buns.

4. Students make a verbal presentation about the celebration and then perform the dances they have created or re-created. (Safety tip: Candles should be unlit.)

### Grades 9 to 12

1. Students research Native American holidays. They incorporate them into a huge festival (powwow).

2. Invite Native American dancers to come to the class and demonstrate some traditional dances and movements. Their visit could take the form of a lecture-demonstration.

3. Students then take the steps they learned and create their own dances based on the traditional steps and movements. The music classes could provide drumming, or students in the dance classes could take turns drumming and chanting.

4. When you have several dances from several classes, the students could invite the community to a powwow. For this celebration

they could prepare short verbal and visual presentations about the different tribes and what their dances represent. Students could take this presentation to the elementary grades.

## Criteria for Assessment

The students' work of the Holiday Dance activity should include the following criteria:

### Movement Skills

- ✓ Use of the body as an instrument for expression and communication through movement
- ✓ Use of movement elements and skills
- ✓ A series of movements to form movement patterns
- ✓ Addition to personal movement vocabulary
- ✓ Representation of a story line through movement
- ✓ Variation of the quality of movement through change of expression
- ✓ Memorization of a dance learned outside of class

### Cognitive Skills

- ✓ Observation skills
- ✓ Memorization of a sequence of movements
- ✓ Persistence with a task
- ✓ Constructive comments
- ✓ Application of decision-making skills
- ✓ Translation of movement into words
- ✓ Use of interviewing techniques
- ✓ Evidence of research included in written work and performance
- ✓ Evidence of understanding of cultures and how cultures are influenced by religion, customs, and tradition

### Choreographic and Creative Process

- ✓ Variation of original combination while exploring movement
- ✓ Interpretation of choreographic concepts used to express ideas nonverbally through dance
- ✓ Representation through movements to portray words, thoughts, and ideas
- ✓ Evidence of own ideas in dance making

## Social and Aesthetic Skills
✓ Self-direction and self-discipline

✓ Contribution to the group effort

✓ Performance of the finished combination or dance phrase

✓ Observation of others' performances

✓ Constructive comments

✓ Sense of accomplishment

✓ Evidence of an increased cultural awareness

When assessing students, base your assessment for this activity on these criteria, or use the sample checklists or assessment forms in chapter 6. A general rubric that can be used for evaluating students' work follows.

3 = Above standard. Completed all "Try This" suggestions.

Completed all challenges.

Completed "Ask Yourself" in written form.

2 = At standard. Completed all "Try This" suggestions.

Completed one of the challenges.

Answered "Ask Yourself" in discussion form.

1 = Needs more work. Missing any criteria from the "at standard" level.

# Out of This World

This activity fulfills the following standards:
    National Dance Standards: 1, 2, 3, 4, 7
    National Standards for Physical Education: 1, 2, 5, 6

The solar system is full of movement, such as elliptical orbits, spinning rotations, shooting comets, explosions of the solar flares, and growing and waning spots on Jupiter. Dance activities can bring life and deeper meaning to a science unit on the solar system.

## Description of Activity or Procedure

After doing research on the solar system, decide which aspects of the research best lend themselves to inspiring movement. Create movements that represent these ideas. Organize them into a dance about the solar system.

## Sample Activity

Look at a diagram of the different orbits (sizes, shapes, and placements in the solar system). Create a floor pattern (pathway) based on these orbits. Use different locomotor movement combinations for each floor pattern. Assign a group of students to perform each orbit dance.

## Grade Level Suggestions
## for Creating Out of This World Dance

Out of This World can be adapted to any age level by varying the presentation and organization of the material. Suggestions for modifications follow.

### Grades K to 4

1. Create a locomotor phrase with a group of students who will represent explorers of the solar system.
2. Have groups of students create movement phrases to represent the distinguishing characteristics of each planet (Mercury having the smallest and fastest orbit, Venus with cloud cover that reflects sunlight to make it the brightest planet in our sky, Earth with its

great amount of water, Mars as a red desert). Make sure to include appropriate shapes and nonlocomotor and locomotor movements. Also, have a group of students dance the explorer part. These students should use different movements to get from planet to planet.

3. Have the students create a story line that describes explorers visiting each planet, using the explorer group as transitions between planet dances. Try using Gustav Holst's work *The Planets* as musical accompaniment.

### Grades 5 to 8

1. Assign a group of students to read a portion of a science book about the solar system. Have them list all the verbs and descriptive words in each section of the text.

2. Use these verbs and descriptive words to create a movement phrase. The verbs should describe the planets' movements, and the descriptive words help students determine how these movements are done.

3. Organize these movement phrases into a dance about the solar system.

### Grades 9 to 12

1. Have the students research the forces (gravity, mass, inertia, velocity) that cause planets and other bodies from outer space to move and that also hold the solar system together.

2. Assign small groups of students to find ways to define or illustrate, in movement phrases, the terms that they found in their research.

3. Have these groups also create a spoken text about their assigned term and combine it with their movement definitions (dance phrases).

## Criteria for Assessment

The students' work of the Out of this World activity should include the following criteria:

### Movement Skills

✓ Use of the body as an instrument for expression and communication through movement

✓ Use of movement elements and skills

✓ A series of movements to form movement patterns

✓ Addition to personal movement vocabulary

✓ Representation of a story line through movement

✓ Variation of the quality of movement through change of expression

## Cognitive Skills

✓ Observation skills

✓ Memorization of a sequence of movements

✓ Persistence with a task

✓ Constructive comments

✓ Application of decision-making skills

✓ Translation of movement into words

✓ Evidence of research included in written work and performance

## Choreographic and Creative Process

✓ Variation of original combination while exploring movement

✓ Interpretation of choreographic concepts used to express ideas nonverbally through dance

✓ Representation through movements to portray words, thoughts, and ideas

✓ Evidence of own ideas in dance making

## Social and Aesthetic Skills

✓ Self-direction and self-discipline

✓ Contribution to the group effort

✓ Performance of the finished combination or dance phrase

✓ Observation of others' performances

✓ Constructive comments

✓ Sense of accomplishment

When assessing students, base your assessment for this activity on these criteria, or use the sample checklists or assessment forms in chapter 6. A general rubric that can be used for evaluating students' work follows.

3 = Above standard. Completed all "Try This" suggestions.
   Completed all challenges.
   Completed "Ask Yourself" in written form.
2 = At standard. Completed all "Try This" suggestions.
   Completed one of the challenges.
   Answered "Ask Yourself" in discussion form.
1 = Needs more work. Missing any criteria from the "at standard" level.

# Four Seasons

This activity fulfills the following standards:
  National Dance Standards: 1, 2, 3, 4, 7
  National Standards for Physical Education: 1, 2, 5, 6

Celebrate the four seasons and the cycles of life through this dance-making activity. Students can communicate various qualities of movement through exploration of the idea of four seasons.

## Description of Activity or Procedure

Brainstorm or research the four seasons of the year: winter, spring, summer, and fall. For each season, develop movement that represents words or ideas chosen from the research. Link these four sections of movement together for a whole dance.

## Sample Activity

Have the students brainstorm the different activities that people can do in spring, summer, fall, and winter (examples are flying kites, swimming, bobbing for apples, and skiing, respectively). Divide the students into four groups and assign a season to each or have them choose a season. Have each group create and combine movements for the seasonal activities. Let each group perform in the order of spring, summer, fall, and winter.

## Grade Level Suggestions
## for Creating Four Seasons Dance

Four Seasons can be adapted to any age level by varying the presentation and organization of the material. Suggestions for modifications follow.

### Grades K to 4
1. Discuss the life cycle of flowering plants during the four seasons: sprouting, flowering, drying up, and seeding and sleeping roots.

2. Have students create movements to represent each of these ideas. Use low, middle, and high levels for sprouting. Use props to represent flowers such as dandelions and tiger lilies (lion and tiger masks), sunflowers (sunglasses), bell-shaped lilies of the valley (bells), and snapdragons (dragon tails). Use wide shapes and movements going to narrow shapes and movements for drying up, and use scattering movements for seeding. Use pantomime and abstraction to show going to sleep for the winter. Remember that pantomime is very literal. When you make an abstraction from the literal, the movements are symbolic and less realistic and less mimicking; this is the beginning of dance movement.

3. Put the sections in order. Practice. Perform and share.

## Grades 5 to 8

1. Get prints of Pieter Bruegel's paintings that represent the four seasons.

2. Divide students into groups, or have them choose their favorite seasons or paintings. Have students draw or write down shapes, designs, ideas, and thoughts that they see or that occur to them as they look at the paintings.

3. Students should create movements based on their research. Have them put movements together to form dance phrases and then put the dance phrases together to form sections of a dance representing each season.

4. Choose favorite movements from each season's section and put them together for a finale.

## Grades 9 to 12

1. Have students reflect on the cycles of life (birth and baby years, childhood, adulthood, and old age) and how they correspond to the seasons of the year.

2. Have the students develop a general movement phrase using shapes and locomotor and nonlocomotor movements. For each of the stages, change how this movement phrase is done to represent the four stages of life.

3. Use costume pieces to portray each stage of life. Practice. Perform and share.

## Criteria for Assessment

The students' work of the Four Seasons activity should include the following criteria:

### Movement Skills

✓ Use of the body as an instrument for expression and communication through movement

✓ Use of movement elements and skills

✓ A series of movements to form movement patterns

✓ Addition to personal movement vocabulary

✓ Representation of a story line through movement

✓ Variation of the quality of movement through change of expression

### Cognitive Skills

✓ Observation skills

✓ Memorization of a sequence of movements

✓ Persistence with a task

✓ Constructive comments

✓ Application of decision-making skills

✓ Translation of movement into words

✓ Use of interviewing techniques

✓ Evidence of research included in written work and performance

### Choreographic and Creative Process

✓ Variation of original combination while exploring movement

✓ Interpretation of choreographic concepts used to express ideas nonverbally through dance

✓ Representation through movements to portray words, thoughts, and ideas

✓ Evidence of own ideas in dance making

### Social and Aesthetic Skills

✓ Self-direction and self-discipline

✓ Contribution to the group effort

✓ Performance of the finished combination or dance phrase

✓ Observation of others' performances

✓ Constructive comments

✓ Sense of accomplishment

When assessing students, base your assessment for this activity on these criteria, or use the sample checklists or assessment forms in chapter 6. A general rubric that can be used for evaluating students' work follows.

3 = Above standard. Completed all "Try This" suggestions.

 Completed all challenges.

 Completed "Ask Yourself" in written form.

2 = At standard. Completed all "Try This" suggestions.

 Completed one of the challenges.

 Answered "Ask Yourself" in discussion form.

1 = Needs more work. Missing any criteria from the "at standard" level.

# Animal Kingdom

This activity fulfills the following standards:
National Dance Standards: 1, 2, 3, 4, 7
National Standards for Physical Education: 1, 2, 5, 6

The animal kingdom, of which we are a part, is amazing. Fish, birds, mammals, reptiles, amphibians, and insects are all part of the animal kingdom and call Earth their home. Dance activities can facilitate a deeper understanding of all creatures great and small.

## Description of Activity or Procedure

After doing research on the animal kingdom, students decide which aspects of the research they might want to use for the dance-making activities. For example, research might focus on one classification, such as insects, or groups of students might choose different categories.

## Sample Activity

Using research, have students answer the question *What makes a fish a fish?* Have students create small dances that demonstrate their understanding of this question. Repeat this exercise with each classification. Combine all the dances to create an Animal Kingdom Dance.

## Grade Level Suggestions for Creating Animal Kingdom Dance

Animal Kingdom can be adapted to any age level by varying the presentation and organization of the material. Suggestions for modifications follow.

### Grades K to 4

1. After discussing the vastness of the animal kingdom (fish, birds, mammals, reptiles, amphibians, and insects), have students bring in pictures of or research materials for their favorite animals in each category. Research should focus on the question *How does*

*this animal move?* Research material can come from favorite books, videos, the Internet, and interviews with family members or experts.

2. Collect and put into categories all the research materials.

3. Using the combined research material, groups of students should choose four animals and create movement phrases that demonstrate their understanding of how the various animals move.

4. Organize these different animal movement phrases to make a dance. You and your students can determine the order of which movements come first and what would make a great finish.

5. Have students create animal masks that they use when performing their dances.

## Grades 5 to 8

1. Have students brainstorm stories that use animals as main characters, or have them bring in these stories.

2. Discuss how animal characteristics are represented in the various stories, such as sly fox, hungry bear, and mean old wolf. Have the students decide whether or not these characteristics are based on fact.

3. Choose six animals that are represented in stories. Have the students write paragraphs that illustrate the individual qualities of each animal. Create a movement signature for each animal that portrays their unique qualities.

4. Create both an original story that uses all six characters and a dance based on this story.

## Grades 9 to 12

1. Have students develop a series of questions about the following: animal migration patterns, humans' effect on animals, and the food chain.

2. Choose one of the topics to research. The research should answer the student-generated questions.

3. Have the students develop a series of dances that explain the chosen topic. Use these dances as part of a lecture-demonstration for elementary school children.

## Criteria for Assessments

The students' work of the Animal Kingdom activity should include the following criteria:

### Movement Skills

✓ Use of the body as an instrument for expression and communication through movement

✓ Use of movement elements and skills

✓ A series of movements to form movement patterns

✓ Addition to personal movement vocabulary

✓ Representation of a story line through movement

✓ Variation of the quality of movement through change of expression

### Cognitive Skills

✓ Observation skills

✓ Memorization of a sequence of movements

✓ Persistence with a task

✓ Constructive comments

✓ Application of decision-making skills

✓ Translation of movement into words

✓ Use of interviewing techniques

✓ Evidence of research included in written work and performance

### Choreographic and Creative Process

✓ Variation of original combination while exploring movement

✓ Interpretation of choreographic concepts used to express ideas nonverbally through dance

✓ Representation through movements to portray words, thoughts, and ideas

✓ Evidence of own ideas in dance making

### Social and Aesthetic Skills

✓ Self-direction and self-discipline

✓ Contribution to the group effort

✓ Performance of the finished combination or dance phrase

✓ Observation of others' performances

✓ Constructive comments

✓ Sense of accomplishment

✓ Appreciation of others and their feelings

When assessing students, base your assessment for this activity on these criteria, or use the sample checklists or assessment forms in chapter 6. A general rubric that can be used for evaluating students' work follows.

3 = Above standard. Completed all "Try This" suggestions.

   Completed all challenges.

   Completed "Ask Yourself" in written form.

2 = At standard. Completed all "Try This" suggestions.

   Completed one of the challenges.

   Answered "Ask Yourself" in discussion form.

1 = Needs more work. Missing any criteria from the "at standard" level.

# It's All Around Us

This activity fulfills the following standards:
National Dance Standards: 1, 2, 3, 4, 7
National Standards for Physical Education: 1, 2, 5, 6

Environment is the circumstances or conditions that surround any given thing. All living beings are influenced in some way by their environments. This concept can be used to create many different and interesting dances.

## Description of Activity or Procedure

Have the students brainstorm types of environments such as habitats, climate-related environments, school environment, and cultural environment. Have the students research these various meanings of the word *environment.* Help the students create movements that represent aspects of a specific environment and combine them to illustrate that environment.

## Sample Activity

Imagine life on a tropical island. Brainstorm conditions in that environment that would affect you adversely. Create a dance that represents your reaction to these adverse conditions.

## Grade Level Suggestions for Creating It's All Around Us

It's All Around Us can be adapted to any age level by varying the presentation and organization of the material. Suggestions for modifications follow.

### Grades K to 4
1. Discuss the following habitats: ocean, coast, river, bog, grassland, forest, desert, polar regions.
2. Students should draw a picture or write a paragraph describing one of these habitats.
3. Let the students create movements that illustrate characteristics of this environment. Two examples are shaking motions showing that it is cold, and movements that demonstrate freezing and thawing.

4. Combine the movements to create a dance about that environment.

## Grades 5 to 8

1. Have students brainstorm ways that humans are affecting the environment. Students should research some of these ideas. Use this research to create a dance that demonstrates humans' negative effect on the environment and how we can correct it.

2. Create a dance that shows our environment as it should be. This will be section A of the dance.

3. Create movements that portray some of the destructive things that we do to our environment and how we can fix those things. This will be section B of the dance.

4. Create a dance using ABA choreographic form.

## Grades 9 to 12

1. Have the students brainstorm on the physical characteristics of a fictitious environment.

2. Have the students create movement phrases that illustrate the various aspects of the environment.

3. Have the students create different movement phrases that suggest some type of conflict that threatens to change the environment.

4. Have the students demonstrate with more movement phrases ways to resolve the conflict.

5. By linking these movement phrases together in a timeline, students create a dance that shows these possible solutions to environmental conflicts.

## Criteria for Assessment

The students' work in the It's All Around Us activity should include the following criteria:

### Movement Skills

    ✓ Use of the body as an instrument for expression and communication through movement

    ✓ Use of movement elements and skills

    ✓ A series of movements to form movement patterns

    ✓ Addition to personal movement vocabulary

    ✓ Representation of a story line through movement

    ✓ Variation of the quality of movement through change of expression

## Cognitive Skills

- ✓ Observation skills
- ✓ Memorization of a sequence of movements
- ✓ Persistence with a task
- ✓ Constructive comments
- ✓ Application of decision-making skills
- ✓ Translation of movement into words
- ✓ Use of interviewing techniques
- ✓ Evidence of research included in written work and performance

## Choreographic and Creative Process

- ✓ Variation of original combination while exploring movement
- ✓ Interpretation of choreographic concepts used to express ideas nonverbally through dance
- ✓ Representation through movements to portray words, thoughts, and ideas
- ✓ Evidence of own ideas in dance making

## Social and Aesthetic Skills

- ✓ Self-direction and self-discipline
- ✓ Contribution to the group effort
- ✓ Performance of the finished combination or dance phrase
- ✓ Observation of others' performances
- ✓ Constructive comments
- ✓ Sense of accomplishment

When assessing students, base your assessment for this activity on these criteria, or use the sample checklists or assessment forms in chapter 6. A general rubric that can be used for evaluating students' work follows.

3 = Above standard. Completed all "Try This" suggestions.
   Completed all challenges.
   Completed "Ask Yourself" in written form.
2 = At standard. Completed all "Try This" suggestions.
   Completed one of the challenges.
   Answered "Ask Yourself" in discussion form.
1 = Needs more work. Missing any criteria from the "at standard" level.

# Summary

The activities in this chapter introduce the basics of choreography, but they are by no means comprehensive. However, the activities should give students an appreciation of the bigger picture of dance education, a place where they have creative input and a sense of ownership. In many cases an activity may be the spark that ignites the flame of curiosity, making a student more likely to seek formal, intensive, and long-term dance education.

# National Standards

## National Dance Content Standards

**Standard 1:**   Identifying and demonstrating movement elements and skills in performing dance.

**Standard 2:**   Understanding choreographic principles, processes, and structures.

**Standard 3:**   Understanding dance as a way to create and communicate meaning.

**Standard 4:**   Applying and demonstrating critical and creative thinking skills in dance.

**Standard 5:**   Demonstrating and understanding dance in various cultures and historical periods.

**Standard 6:**   Making connections between dance and healthful living.

**Standard 7:**   Making connections between dance and other disciplines.

National Dance Standards 1-7 (pp. 6-9) These quotes are reprinted from *The National Standards for Arts Education* with permission of the National Dance Association (NDA), an association of the American Alliance for Health, Physical Education, Recreation, and Dance. The source of the National Dance Standards *(National Standards for Dance Education: What Every Young American Should Know and Be Able to Do in Dance)* may be purchased from: National Dance Association, 1900 Association Drive, Reston, VA 20191-1599; or telephone (703) 476-3421.

# National Standards for Physical Education

The physically educated person:

**Standard 1:** Demonstrates competency in motor skills and movement patterns needed to perform a variety of physical activities.

**Standard 2:** Demonstrates understanding of movement concepts, principles, strategies, and tactics as they apply to the learning and performance of physical activities.

**Standard 3:** Participates regularly in physical activity

**Standard 4:** Achieves and maintains a health-enhancing level of physical fitness.

**Standard 5:** Exhibits responsible personal and social behavior that respects self and others in physical activity settings.

**Standard 6:** Values physical activity for health, enjoyment, challenge, self-expression, and/or social interaction.

# GLOSSARY

In many instances the terms for dance steps and movement skills are different while the actual steps and procedures are similar. This glossary introduces these steps and skills with everyday terms but also includes correct dance terms and pronunciation. Familiarity with these terms can become part of class vocabulary.

## Foot Positions (General Dance) (see figure G.1)

**first position**—Feet are parallel and slightly apart.

**second position**—Feet are parallel and about a foot-width apart.

**fourth position**—Feet are parallel, one foot ahead of the other, and about a foot-width apart.

**Figure G.1** Foot positions: *(a)* first, *(b)* second, and *(c)* fourth.

## Foot Positions (Ballet) (see figure G.2)

**first position**—Heels touch. Toes are turned out. The ideal aim is to make a straight line with the feet, although this is not always possible.

**second position**—Heels are about 12 inches apart. Toes are turned out, and weight is evenly distributed on each foot.

**third position**—Feet are touching. Heel of right foot is in front of arch of left foot, and toes are turned out. Position can also be reversed.

**fourth position**—Right foot is about 10 inches in front of left foot. Hips are aligned and facing forward, and toes are turned out. Position can also be reversed.

**fifth position**—Feet are touching. Heel of right foot is in front of left toe, and toes are turned out. Position can also be reversed.

**FIGURE G.2**    Ballet foot positions: *(a)* first, *(b)* second, *(c)* third, *(d)* fourth, and *(e)* fifth.

## Arm Positions (Ballet)

**first position**—Arms are rounded and low in the front of your body.

**second position**—Arms are up just below shoulder level and to the sides of your body.

**third position**—One arm is rounded in front of your body, and the other is extended to the side, as in second position. The arm in front of your body can be at any level.

**fourth position**—One arm is rounded above your head, and the other is rounded in front of your body.

**fifth position**—Both arms are rounded and almost touching. They can be low, just below shoulder level, or over your head.

## Body Positions

The following are basic body positions for dance, gymnastics, and general physical education. They can be used in building a dance, in warm-ups and cool-downs, in starting positions, or in general exercise.

**flat back**—Used in modern and jazz disciplines. Feet are parallel and slightly apart. Body is at a 90-degree angle to the legs, bending from the hips, with no curve of the spine (also called a pike position) (see figure G.3).

**layout**—Stand with feet together and arms stretched overhead. Body and elbows are straight.

**lunge**—Legs are in a stride stance. One leg is stretched behind your body, with the knee straight and toes pointed. The arms can be in any prescribed position (see figure G.4).

**Figure G.3**  Flat back.

**Figure G.4**  Lunge.

**scale** or **arabesque**—One leg is lifted behind your body, with the knee straight and toes pointed. The arms can be in any prescribed position.

**stag**—Lift one leg to the front, side, or back, keeping the knee bent at a right angle (also called an attitude position) (see figure G.5).

**straddle**—Stand with both feet on the floor in parallel position in a wide stance.

**stride**—Feet are in a stationary walking position.

**tuck**—Knees and chest are pulled in to each other.

**Figure G.5**  Attitude or stag.

## Dance-Building Movements

The following terms are used when building a dance or executing a warm-up, either supported at a barre or unsupported in the center of the room. If a wall-mounted or portable barre is not available, then the back of a chair or a waist-high ledge can also be used for support.

**accented ankle beats without extensions** or **battement battu** [baht-MAHN ba-TEW]—Same as ankle beats without extensions, accenting with the working leg pausing either in front or in back.

**ankle beats without extensions** or **battement serré** [baht-MAHN seh-RAY]—With your foot at the top of the ankle of the supporting leg (sur le cou-de-pied), move the leg from the front of the ankle to the back. This movement can be done quickly, but the knee must remain turned out.

**arm movements** or **port de bras** [por duh brah]—Carriage of the arms, usually involving the body bending and stretching forward, side, or back.

**circular move of the leg** or **rond de jambe à terre** [rawn duh zhahm ah TEHR]—This exercise helps your leg turn out at the hip joint. Your body and supporting leg should remain still while your working leg moves around to the back in a half-circle pattern with the leg fully extended and the toe fully pointed (see figure G.6). For outside (en dehors), start with the leg moving forward first and then around in the half circle. For inside (en dedans), start with the leg moving behind and then out to the side and around to the front.

**double strike** or **double frappé** [frah-PAY]—Same as strike except that the working leg beats around the ankle before it extends out. Starting from back to front or vice versa, the working heel touches the ankle of the supporting leg twice before it extends out.

**foot brush** or **battement dégagé** [baht-MAHN day-ga-ZHAY] or **glissé** [glee-SAY]—This move is the same as pointed foot (tendu [tahn-DEW]) except that the foot leaves the floor, and it is done rather sharply.

**Figure G.6**   Circle move of the leg.

**deep knee bend** or **grand plié** [grahn plee-AY]—Bend your knees, keeping your heels on the floor for as long as possible and then letting them lift off. Come up to the original position. In second position, the heels stay on the ground, and you do not go all the way down (see figure G.7). *Note:* Student should assume correct posture with spine aligned. As the knees bend and the body lowers, the student should carry the weight in the thighs and should not sink to the floor. The buttocks should not come to rest on the heels and calves. When beginning the rise out of the bend, the student should push the heels down firmly, again placing the weight in the thighs. The back should be straight. This method takes all strain off the knee joints. Very young children do not have the musculature to execute this properly; therefore, the teaching of a deep knee bend or grand plié should not begin until the child is approximately 8 years old.

**knee bend** or **demi-plié** [deh-MEE plee-AY]—Bend your knees sideways over your toes and move back to your original position. Your heels should stay on the ground, and the movement should be as smooth as possible.

**Figure G.7**   Pliés: *(a)* grand and *(b)* demi.

**kick, leg raise,** or **grand battement** [grahn bat-MAHN]—Throw the leg up (kick) to front, side, or back. The leg goes through the extended point (tendu [tahn-DEW]) position on the way up and on the way down. The knee is straight and the toes are extended in a pointed position. The foot may flex after it has left the floor (see figure G.8).

**pointed foot** or **battement tendu** [baht-MAHN tahn-DEW]—Slide your foot along the floor from first or fifth position to an extended point to the front, side, or back (devant, à la seconde, or derrière). Then slide it back to the original position. The tip of the big toe should not leave the floor.

**rise** or **relevé** [reh-luh-VAY]—Rising up to half-point (demi-pointe) in any position either on one foot or two.

**stable ankle beats** or **petit battement** [puh-TEE baht-MAHN]—Same as accented ankle beats without extensions except that the toe of the working leg only taps in front of the ankle of the supporting leg. There is no action from the knee up, and the working ankle is stable.

**strike** or **battement frappé** [baht-MAHN frah-PAY]—This exercise strengthens your leg and foot. Starting with the heel of the working leg placed above the ankle of the supporting leg (sur le cou-de-pied), strike the floor with the ball of your working leg, extending the leg fully with pointed toes. Return the foot to the original position, keeping it flexed. Keep the thigh still and the knee turned out (see figure G.9). This exercise can be done to the front, side, or back. It can also be done with the supporting leg on half-point (demi-pointe).

**FIGURE G.8**   Kick.

**FIGURE G.9**   Strike.

## Jumping and Turning Steps

The following terms are used when executing steps and combinations of steps in varied patterns or alone using a variety of space and direction. This basic dance vocabulary can be used to build a dance. However, there are many more words in the dance vocabulary. The terms and the execution of the steps mentioned here would be exacting if done in a formal dance class, but in this instance a reasonable facsimile gives the desired effect.

Steps that leave the floor are divided into three categories:

- **jump**—Leave the floor from two feet and land in the same position.
- **hop**—The action starts and finishes on the same foot.
- **leap**—The weight is transferred from one foot to another.

**big leap** or **grand jeté** [grahn zhuh-TAY]—A leap through the air with the legs in a stretched position. The front or back leg can be bent in a stag position for variation.

**foot exchange** or **changement** [shahnzh-MAHN]—Start with feet in ballet fifth position. After doing a knee bend (demi-plié), jump off the floor and exchange feet in the air so that you land with the other foot in front. Toes should be pointed while you are in the air, and knees should be straight. Land in a knee bend (demi-plié).

**Jump with full, half,** or **quarter turn** or **tour en l'air** [toor ahn LEHR]—This move is a combination of a jump step and turn step. Start with both feet on the floor and knees bent (demi-plié). Jump, lifting both feet off the floor and rotating in a single direction.

**gallop** or **chassé** [shah-SAY]—A sliding step that feels like a gallop but with pointed and turned-out feet.

**glide** or **glissade** [glee-SAHD]—This move starts in fifth position and in a knee bend (demi-plié). Brush (dégagé) the foot to second position (or to the front or back) lightly, then transfer the weight from the standing foot to the foot that has just lifted off the floor. Close the other foot to fifth position. This move can be done forward (en avant), side (à la seconde), or back (derrière). It is technically classified as a small leap.

**hop** or **temps levé** [tahn luh-VAY]—This move is a spring or hop on one foot with the raised leg in any position.

**jump** or **sauté** [soh-TAY]—Although the word means to jump, it applies specifically to a jump that starts and finishes in the same position, such as first or second (see figure G.10).

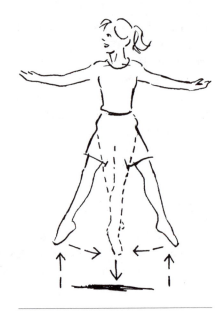

**Figure G.10**  Jump.

**Figure G.11**  Jumping jack.

**jumping jack** or **échappé sauté** [ay-shah-PAY soh-TAY]—Starting in fifth or first position, jump to second position, landing in a knee bend (demi-plié) and springing back up and closing to fifth or first position (see figure G.11).

**leg beats in the air, bell click,** or **cabriole** [kah-bree-AWL]—While standing on one foot, brush (dégagé) the other foot in any direction. Lift up off the floor in a hop or temps levé. At the top of the jump, beat or click legs together; open them as you come down, and land on one foot in a knee bend (demi-plié). Legs can be bent or straight in the air. When legs are bent, click your heels. When legs are straight in the air, beat your calves or thighs.

**one-foot turn, whirl,** or **pirouette** [peer-WHET]

• **outside** or **en dehors** [ahn duh-OR]—Prepare by pointing (tendu) the right foot to the side, and place foot in back in fourth position with weight evenly distributed. Right arm is in front and left arm is to the side. At the same time open the right arm, raise the right leg, which is bent at the knee and touching the supporting leg with the toe (piqué position), and rise up (relevé) on the left leg

**Figure G.12**  One-foot turn.      **Figure G.13**  Run and leap.

and make a revolution to the right. Plan to end in fifth position (see figure G.12).

- **inside** or **en dedans [ahn duh-DAHN]**—Prepare by pointing (tendu) the right foot to the side, and place foot in back in fourth position with weight evenly distributed. Left arm is in front and right arm is to the side. At the same time open the left arm, raise the right leg, which is bent at the knee and touching the supporting leg with the toe (piqué position), and rise up (relevé) on the left leg and make a revolution to the left. Plan to end in fifth position.

**pivot on one foot** or **promenade** [prah-muh-NAHD]—Stand on one foot with the other leg lifted off the floor. Make a circular move by pivoting the heel of the standing foot, rotating in the same direction until you complete the desired number of revolutions.

**prance** or **emboité** [ahn-bwah-TAY]—This move shifts weight from one leg to another. Start with one foot off the floor and the standing leg bent. Spring up and land on the raised foot (bent knee) with the other foot now lifted off the floor in the desired position.

**run and leap** or **pas de couru** [pah duh koo-REW], **grande jeté**—Take three running steps and execute a giant leap (see figure G.13).

**scissors jump** or **sissonne** [see-SAWN]—Start with both feet on the floor in a knee bend (demi-plié). Jump off with both feet, pushing weight to one leg and landing on that one leg in a knee bend (demi-plié) (see figure G.14).

**seat turn** or **sit spin**—Sit on the floor, rotating on the buttocks with feet in desired position. You can propel the turn gradually by pushing slowly with hands or by a big push to start.

**three-step turn** or **chaîné** [sheh-NAY]—This turn is a chain going from second position facing forward to second position facing backward. As you begin, the arms are open to second position when you face forward, and they're closed to middle fifth when you face backwards. You keep rotating in the same direction, not back and forth like a washing machine.

**turning steps**—The body makes circular moves around an axis.

**wrap turn** or **soutenu** [soota-NEW]—Wrap one foot around the other tightly, and rotate your body in the direction of the standing foot, slowly unwrapping your feet and ending in fifth position (see figure G.15).

**FIGURE G.14**   Scissors jump.        **FIGURE G.15**   Wrap turn.

## Linking Steps

These series of steps can be termed "linking" steps because they can be used to join other steps and movements.

**little steps** or **bourrée** [boo-RAY]—Feet are closed in a tight fifth position. Take tiny steps in any direction (working to keep the feet almost together). This step can also be done as a turn in place.

**pas de basque** [pah duh BAHSK]—Start in first position. Step to second position with right foot. Bring left foot in front to fourth position. Slide right foot to left foot into fifth position. This step can be reversed or done while moving backward. It is often used in European folk dancing and can also be done with a leap from the first step to the second.

**pas de bourrée** [pah duh boo-RAY]—Start with right foot raised behind left ankle (coupé position). With the right foot step back behind you to fourth position, and with the left foot step to second position. With the right foot step forward to fourth position and lift the back leg to touch the ankle of the front leg (coupé position). You may also close to fifth position on the final step (see figure G.16).

**thank you** or **révérence** [reh-vuh-RAHNS]—A bow, usually at the end of class, to thank the teacher, done in any fashion.

**waltz, triplet**—Move weight onto one foot with knee bent into a demi-plié. Reach out with the other foot onto half-point or ball of the foot (demi-pointe). Do the same with the first foot. This completes one waltz, which is then continued in any direction or while turning.

**Figure G.16**  Pas de bourrée.

## Directional and Descriptive Terms

These words may be used to describe how a dance movement should be performed.

**à la seconde** [ah lah suh-COHND]—to the side.

**bound movement**—Very controlled movement.

**contra dancing**—Dances in which two lines are facing.

**coupé** [koo-PAY] **position**—With working foot touching front or back of supporting ankle.

**demi-pointe**—Half-point, on the ball of the foot.

**derrière** [deh-ree-YEHR]—To the back.

**devant** [duh-VAHN]—To the front.

**en avant** [ah nah-VAHN]—Forward.

**en dedans** [ahn duh-DAHN]—To the inside.

**en dehors** [ahn duh-OR]—To the outside.

**free movement**—Open, spontaneous movement.

**piqué** [pee-KAY]—The working leg is bent at the knee, with the toe touching the supporting leg.

**sur le cou-de-pied** [sewr luh KOO duh peeYAY]—Literally, "on the instep." The heel of the working leg is placed above the ankle of the supporting leg.

**tendu** [tahn-DEW]—Literally, "stretched." With leg extended or pointed.

## Dance Terms

**choreography**—The art of building dances.

**movement pattern**—The configuration of several movements.

**three parts of a dance**—The beginning, the middle, and the end.

# ABOUT THE AUTHORS

**Susan McGreevy-Nichols** is the national director of Arts, Planning and School Support for the Galef Institute in Los Angeles. She taught at Roger Williams Middle School in Providence, Rhode Island, from 1974 to 2002. She was the founder and director of the inner-city school's nationally recognized dance program in which more than 300 of the school's 900 students elected to participate.

Susan is coauthor of *Building Dances: A Guide to Putting Movements Together* (1995) and its second edition (in press), *Building More Dances: Blueprints for Putting Movements Together* (2001), and *Dance About Anything* (in press). She is a charter member and presenter of the National Dance Education Organization (NDEO) and a former treasurer and board member. She also has served as the president of the National Dance Association (NDA) and the nominating chair and (Rhode Island) state leader for the Kennedy Center Alliance for Arts Education.

Susan has received numerous NDA presidential citations and an Eastern District Association (EDA) of the American Alliance of Health, Physical Education, Recreation and Dance (AAHPERD) Merit Award in Dance. In 1994 she was named Rhode Island's Dance Teacher of the Year, and in 1995 she was honored both as the NDA National Dance Teacher of the Year and as an EDA Outstanding Professional. She received AAHPERD's Honor Award in 2000.

**Helene Scheff, RDE,** has been a dance educator and administrator for 45 years in both the public and private sectors. She is coauthor of *Building Dances: A Guide to Putting Movements Together* (1995), *Building More Dances: Blueprints for Putting Movements Together* (2001), *Experiencing Dance: From Student to Dance Artist* (2005), and *Dance About Anything* (in press).

A registered dance educator, Scheff is the founder and executive director of Chance to Dance, an in-school dance program started in 1985 that brings quality dance education to children in grades 4 through 8.

A graduate of the famed NYC High School of Performing Arts, Scheff is a former Joffrey Ballet dancer. She is a founding member and former president of the Dance Alliance of Rhode Island and has served as vice president of dance for the Eastern District Association (EDA) of the American Alliance for Health, Physical Education, Recreation and Dance. She is a board member of the Rhode Island Alliance for Arts Education and the Committee Liaison for UNITY. Scheff is a member of the National Dance Association (NDA) and a charter member of the National Dance Education Organization (NDEO).

Scheff was named the Rhode Island Association for Health, Physical Education, Recreation and Dance's (RIAHPERD) Dance Teacher of the Year in 1996 and was honored as an EDA Outstanding Professional in 1996. She received the RIAHPERD President's Honor Award in 1997 and an NDA Presidential Citation in 1998. She was awarded the Dance Alliance of Rhode Island Dance Legacy Award in 2002.

 **Marty Sprague, MA,** is a professional choreographer and performer with more than 29 years of experience in public dance education. She is the dance teacher at the Providence Academy of International Studies and artistic director of Chance to Dance.

Marty holds a master's degree in dance education from the Teacher's College at Columbia University and a BFA in dance from Boston Conservatory. She has been a licensed trainer for the National Center for Education and the Economy's Course I, Standards-Based Curriculum—a professional development course for standards-based teaching and learning. She served on the Rhode Island Governor's Task Force for Literacy in the Arts. Marty is a member of the Arabella Project, a dance group exploring the realms of the older dancer.

Marty is coauthor of *Building More Dances: Blueprints for Putting Movements Together* (2001), *Experiencing Dance: From Student to Dance Artist* (2005), and *Dance About Anything* (in press). She also served as a consultant to the authors for the first edition of *Building Dances: A Guide to Putting Movements Together* (1995).

In 1992 Marty was named the Rhode Island Dance Educator of the Year and in 1998 earned an Outstanding Professional Award from EDA. In 2004, Marty was honored with Dance Teacher Magazine's Dance Teacher of the Year Award for K-12. She is a member of the National Dance Association (NDA) and the Association for Supervision and Curriculum Development, and she is a charter member of National Dance Education Organization (NDEO).